D0938673

# OVERCOMING OPPOSITION:

*A Survival Manual for Executives*

## Other Books by Philip Lesly

# OVERCOMING OPPOSITION:

*A Survival Manual for Executives*

## Philip Lesly

Prentice-Hall, Inc. Englewood Cliffs, N.J.

Prentice-Hall International, Inc., *London*
Prentice-Hall of Australia, Pty. Ltd., *Sydney*
Prentice-Hall of Canada, Ltd., *Toronto*
Prentice-Hall of India Private Ltd., *New Delhi*
Prentice-Hall of Japan, Inc., *Tokyo*
Prentice-Hall of Southeast Asia Pte. Ltd., *Singapore*
Whitehall Books, Ltd., *Wellington, New Zealand*
Editora Prentice-Hall do Brasil Ltda., *Rio de Janeiro*

**Library of Congress Cataloging in Publication Data**

Lesly, Philip
  Overcoming opposition.

  Includes index.
  1. Activism—defense against.   2. Management—defense of.
3. Pressure groups—United States.   4. Public relations
—United States.   5. Industry—Social aspects—United
States. 6. Executives—United States.   7. Corporate
image—United States.   I. Title.
HD59.2.L47   1984        658.4′062        83-24790
ISBN 0-13-646597-8

Printed in the United States of America

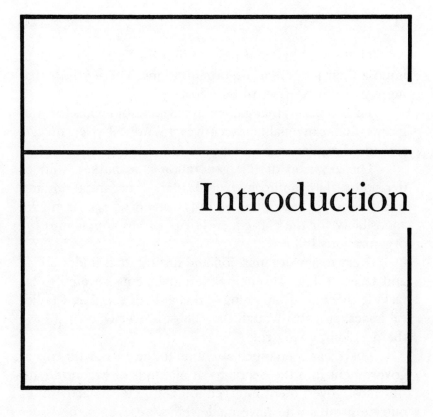

# Introduction

THE FIRST RESPONSIBILITY OF AN EXECUTIVE is to create and maintain orderly procedures. He or she must create order out of many unassimilated elements and facts, and then maintain smooth efficiency in the organization's operations. The effective manager is naturally repelled by disorder and threats to smooth operations.

Yet the trends in North American society seem to be directly contrary to the nature and interest of executives.

Countless external pressures are being formed into groups dedicated to forcing organizations to digress from their orderly procedures. Activist groups advocating many causes seek to impose their wishes on the decision-making of almost all organizations. The phenomenon is so pervading that today's society has been called "The Adversary Culture."

Just one training school, the Midwest Academy in Chicago, trained 10,000 activist organizers between 1973 and 1983.

There is a library of information for those who seek to impose their judgments on organizations. There is little that helps executives offset those efforts.

This book fills that gap and provides guidelines for programs that can enable executives to prevail over unwarranted disruptions.

The key trait of this generation is a marked shift of decision-making authority from leaders of organizations and institutions to those who are outside and who have no responsibility for the consequences of policies and actions the organizations follow.

Every major organization and institution is under attack and faces decline. Disintegrative movements devoted to attacking them are flourishing. The battle of social and political issues, at least through the 1980s, is over who shall have the decision-making role.

There has been much attention to the encroachments of government into the decisions of all kinds of organizations. But most government intervention is due to the activism of outside groups who have made their causes into the issues that government addresses. Other encroachments have been due to activist groups themselves, taking many forms—obstruction, lawsuits, boycotts, pressures on customers and supporters, and so on.

This movement is an attack on leadership. It presumes that all organizations are suspect and that the leaders of those organizations are probably scoundrels or oppressors. Activist dissidents seldom are interested in managing the organizations themselves, and in fact consider to be traitors those among them who move into leadership positions in established organizations. They are anti-leadership and have been strikingly successful in creating public suspicion of leadership of all organizations and institutions.

In modern society, which is dependent on large and complex organizations, the absence of leadership would lead to chaos. So important is leadership that most of history is a chronicle of leaders and their effects. The great world struggle of our time is over the form of leadership, either dictators or elected officials.

So there must be leaders, just as there must be organizations. Each organization has a role to play in the functioning of society.

Leaders are responsible for the organization's results and the consequences of its actions. The functions will still be there, no matter who makes the decisions. So abrogation of decision-making to those who would not be responsible for the results and consequences would lead to the most inhumane of all systems—the opposite of what activists avow they seek.

The future will be shaped largely by how well those who are qualified to be executives in our organizations learn how to deal with this great shift. The conflict between aggressive outsiders and those who seek to fulfill their organizations' responsibilities in an orderly manner will grow.

Every executive and prospective executive needs to fill his or her gap in preparation and experience that creates vulnerability to this new adversary culture.

That is the purpose of this book. It provides insight and facts about the adversarial relationship, and it provides practical help in overcoming opposition, so managers can manage better.

**Philip Lesly**

# CONTENTS

### Section Five—Getting the Desired Result

# OVERCOMING OPPOSITION:

*A Survival Manual for Executives*

# SECTION ONE

# The Threat

# CHAPTER 1

# The Threat
# of
# Dissolution

CHANGES IN THE FLOW OF POWER in the last generation have amounted to a worldwide revolution—quiet but monumental.

It has not been the guns and bombs of the Middle East, Africa, Southeast Asia, and other areas that have been the determining forces of this revolution. It has been a reversal in the nature of power.

Previously, society was organized around strong centralized authority in all institutions, organizations, governments, and other groups. Now it is diffused among nebulous attitudes of millions of individuals. And it is exerted through thousands of groups that constantly shift.

This is a change so pervasive, so complete in transforming how people deal with each other that its real consequences have not yet been realized. And little has been thought through on how it can be dealt with so this new

3

revolution will not bring on the dissolution of human society.

The main effect has been the multiplication of uncertainty. It is ironic that many of the major forces leading to this revolution have been massive steps toward control—control over many life-shortening diseases, famine, the inevitability of drought—and yet the result has been a breakdown of control over human affairs.

The greatest consequence of this massive revolution has been the pervasiveness of uncertainty.

Uncertainty is perhaps the most corrosive of all forces in life. People usually recover from the shock of loss, the indignity of insult, the frustration of failure. But their psychological fiber is worn away when they constantly do not know what to expect—whether they will have sustenance, keep their loved ones, live in comfort or in misery. It is the constant erosion caused by uncertainty that most certainly destroys the human psyche.

The ability to overcome uncertainty has always created the need for power—the power of a hierarchy over its subjects, of the head of a household over a family, of a divine over the flock. The power sets rules and rituals that eliminate the uncertainties. And it is to rid itself of those uncertainties that the group grants the power and agrees to abide by the rules.

In every society there has been such a social contract, whereby structures have assumed the power to define the limits of acceptable actions; and those living within the structures have accepted those limits as a sort of absolutism that holds them together. In that way those outside the group are held at bay, the uncertainties of multiple anarchies within the group are avoided, and the corrosion of uncertainty is alleviated.

Rulers, from tribal chiefs to emperors, have gained obeisance because they have been expected to provide the firm lines of certainty.

That "certainty" may be real or it may take the shape of ritual or superstition.

Religions arise to provide certainties for people who find it intolerable to live with uncertainty about life and the consequence of death.

Universities created administrations and faculties with the power to delineate truth and learning, because their students were ready to invest their youth to help reduce their uncertainties.

People granted physical power to police forces and armies to reduce the uncertainties about their safety and their property.

They gave powers of taxation and control to governments to try to reduce many other uncertainties.

## The Roots of Rules

Around all of these arose the structure of human culture. It set up the rules people lived by almost as though the rules were naturally imprinted on their psyches.

In fact, the overwhelming proportion of what people called "knowledge" before this century was really a combination of codes of conduct.

Religion and theology were sets of commandments, gospels, obeisances, rituals, divine laws, liturgies that firmly established the relationship between the individual and the church—and thereby eliminated uncertainty.

Law and order was a composite of the rules of conduct that everyone must follow—assuring all who accepted them of greater security.

Manners were rules of behavior that "the best people" accepted to assure the proper graces, and apostles such as Emily Post and Amy Vanderbilt made fortunes by laying down the laws of etiquette. Certain things weren't done, by agreement of tradition—no talking when an opponent was about to putt, no chastising the umpire in tennis, no sexual references in mixed company.

All through the era ending with the death of Queen

Victoria, this array of rules and controls prevailed in the visible world—that part of the world that was aware of existence beyond the individual's home village. (Most of humanity still lived in jungles, bush, and desert shut off from "civilization," and so its different rules and laws were non-existent to the Western populace.)

Such a condition continued, with varying changes, throughout most of history because uncertainties were slow to change. It took a long time for invention, science, medicine, or manners to alter, and only a limited number of things were changing at a time. An occasional war or revolution caused upsets that resulted in modifications but they were absorbed like a dollop of chocolate in a gallon of milk, leaving the end product somewhat different but the total substance with essentially the same traits. Events proceeded like a stream that occasionally encountered a rapids or waterfall.

Around the turn of this century all that began to change. As we will see in the next chapter, a whole flood of forces became active. Each was potent in itself. By interacting with each other they forced each factor to change more rapidly and to alter its effect.

Instead of a single stream with an occasional rapids, events became a maelstrom of dozens of streams surging together and embroiling each other's course.

The new pattern was evident in many ways before about 1960, but at that time the relationship of institutions and people was the result of an evolutionary process of thousands of years.

There was always tension between a natural leaning toward the tyranny of those who attained power and a struggle to avert tyranny by the mass of people. It was the opposing tension of these forces that made up societies, and the failure of these tensions to control each other that caused occasional revolutions, regicides, and massacres.

None of the social structures was ideal. In each of them there was grousing among the powerful about the intransigence of the masses at the same time the people bewailed the insensitivity of the rulers. But most of the time societies functioned and most of the time there was moderate progression toward a better role for each individual.

· The Victorian epoch in England and comparable attitudes in other lands marked the apex of authority's domination. Fathers had extreme control over wives and children; each "true religion" asserted its absolutism to its parishioners; police upheld the law rigidly; military officers' hierarchy of power made enlisted personnel almost serfs; in most countries monarchs were still the supreme authority.

These conditions, which had arisen before the railroad, the telegraph, and the mass circulation of books, remained barriers against growing pressures for adjustment.

## Demise of Authority

We have moved in just a few years from a power structure that seemed too rigid to adjust to new conditions, to where all leadership seems helpless to set directions or prevent disruption. All power centers are confronted with activist dissidents.

Governments everywhere can't get policies accepted or decrees carried out. In the United States one-third of the young men required by law to register for the draft refused. The illegal "hidden economy" accounts for perhaps one-fifth of all income.

Thousands of young people whose college educations were made possible by government loans defy the law and the dictates of fairness and refuse repayment. Many of them are in high-paying professions or working for the government, which supposedly is seeking to collect but actually won't use its authority.

A law setting the speed limit at 55 miles per hour to reduce the nation's tribute to Arab countries and to save lives is regarded as a massive affront to liberty and is largely ignored.

Unions can't get their members to accept agreements that their elected leaders have struggled for months to work out. Public employees at the state and local level take jobs knowing it's illegal to strike, and then strike (but federal employees with such restraints were given pause by the President's firing of the air traffic controllers). Injunctions issued by courts are defied—and the first demand of the strikers is that the restrictive law be ignored to give them clemency.

Hundreds of thousands of fathers ignore court orders to pay child support and the courts shrug. Acknowledging that only a small percentage of criminals are caught, police are frustrated even further when judges let most of the crooks go and parole boards let others out long before their short terms are served.

University administrations face rebellions of faculty and students.

Armed forces face massive drug addiction and insubordination.

Corporations are confronted by opposition of employees, communities, consumers, conservationists, environmentalists, minorities, women's groups, clerics, and academics.

In other areas, even repressive nations show the effects. Russia can't hide massive peace marches and hunger-striking citizens. China went through periods of mass refusal to accept dictates that rent the nation.

The extent of the reversal is evidenced by looking at the plaint of a prominent observer of human affairs, Bertrand Russell, who lamented in 1917 the control held by existing institutions:

> Society cannot exist without law and order. . . . But those who are on the side of law and order, since they are reinforced by custom and the instinct for upholding the *status quo*, have no need of a reasoned defense.

Now the opposite condition exists. It is evident on all sides that it is those who defy authority who disclaim any responsibility for their insurgence; and it is the established institution that needs means to defend itself against siege.

## Impact of Multiple Changes

In the past half century there has been an explosion of forces that create change and thereby put massive and multiple pressures on the stability of all organizations and institutions. The complexity of every organization has increased manyfold.

Not long ago, for example, a corporation needed to concern itself only with "the four m's"—materials, manpower, money, and movement of supplies and finished goods. Now the catalogue of materials and sources requires a computer to keep track of it. Manpower is almost half womanpower, includes hundreds of specialties, and is encumbered with thousands of pages of agreements and regulations. Money for financing is such a complex concern that armies of experts are needed. Movement involves not only trains and trucks but air transport and a maze of controls.

And entirely new are concerns about minority hiring, community activism, government intercession, conservationists, environmentalists, militant churchmen, international pressure groups, and more.

Leaders of many organizations find that managing the operation has become a part-time job, giving way to demands of external forces such as these.

The emergence of these external clamors has resulted from a buildup of three groups:

- A mass of people who are freed from the necessities faced by earlier generations to struggle for their needs.

They have the time and the inclination to be perpetual critics.

- A body of professional organizers, who approach issues not from a concern for a particular grievance but in search of a cause they can agitate among other people. Growing up with them has been a whole library of manuals on how to tear down established organizations; and college majors in how to stir groups to assault institutions.

- A coterie of activists in the media who distrust a system that rewards people who deal with practical matters more than it rewards them—and who saw how Woodward and Bernstein converted this attitude into a ticket to wealth and fame.

The emergence of these groups was enhanced by the fertility of the soil in which they grew.

First, they can be simplistic—and it is an axiom that the public will grasp a simple concept while refusing to think about anything that may be complicated. Declaring "No pollution!" has immediate impact and appeal. An explanation of why nothing that humanity needs can be produced without leaving some byproducts that somehow must be disposed of, and there's no known way to do it without either producing some effluent or creating other problems—that's complicated and the public won't pause to hear it.

Second, they can be irresponsible, while the leaders of institutions and organizations are people with great responsibilities, and who, therefore, cannot take irresponsible positions. An activist group can disrupt a city's traffic, causing massive losses of time and money for thousands of people, and face no consequences; or it can spread a lie about the intentions of an organization and face no penalty. The city or the organization, headed by people who probably gained their positions by demonstrating their ability to function responsibly, must function through approved procedures and time-consuming processes.

## Denial of Leadership

Emergence of these counterforces has created a reversal in the role of leadership that often makes it almost impossible to achieve a vital purpose and resolve a mortal threat.

In the past, the most-respected of our leaders took actions they knew they must. There were murmurs of disapproval but their positions as leaders of a nation in peril granted them the tacit authority that overrode presumed restraints.

Lincoln threw people in jail without bail to prevent sabotage of the Union by enemy agents.

Franklin D. Roosevelt quarantined thousands of Japanese-Americans during World War II to prevent pogroms against them and breakdown of wartime order on the West Coast.

Truman dropped the atom bomb on Hiroshima to save many thousands of American lives and prevent dragging out the war; and he began the investigations of potential Communist agents—a step he felt was essential while Stalin was machinating, but which led to Senator Joseph McCarthy.

In today's climate of restriction of all leadership and free license for all critics of our organizations, none of these actions would have been possible. We can only speculate on what life in the Western world would be like today if those actions had not been taken.

The pendulum has swung so far that even the safeguards that have been built into our society over thousands of years to prevent the abuses of power—the body of laws and the independent courts—are also attacked. Dave Dellinger, the Pied Piper of the activists who savaged the 1968 Democratic convention, calls our orderly court procedures "playing the game according to the rules of the oppressors."

Most of history is a chronicle of tyrannies—some benign, some vicious. It is only in our lifetime that as many as ten percent of the people have lived without forced obeisance to monarch, emperor, potentate, or high priest. The first great democracy, ancient Greece, was a democracy for the elite, based on a foundation of slaves. The great Roman civilization was run by emperors and bound together by armed might. The great Chinese civilization was dominated by emperors and lashed into obedience by war lords. That milestone of freedom, the Magna Carta, did not establish the independence of the people but loosened bonds for the barons.

Freedom from tyranny is a new phenomenon—and there is evidence that it may be a brief one. For there is more than one kind of tyranny. What we have known before, and what today's dissidents say they are combating, has been the tyranny of those in power. But it may be replaced by a tyranny of the crowd, in which the assertiveness of groups of people prevents any orderly functioning.

All of history testifies to the evils of tyranny among leaders, from empires to small employers or labor unions. Democracy, when it provides a vehicle for representing the voice and interests of all people, has been proved the best of all formats of social structure. As Winston Churchill said, it is the worst of all systems, except for all the others. But tyranny of the crowd—which prevents representation of the interests of all the people—is not democracy; it is one of "the others."

In America almost no decisions can now be made by Congress, because some assertive group objects to any proposed action. Legislators will not stop giving away the lifeblood of the economy because those who receive scream their opposition.

England watches her past glory sink without letup while noisy groups assert their tyranny over the supposedly elected leadership. Poland's crisis was due not only to the tyranny of Russia's puppets but the tyranny of labor groups that refused to make the working concessions needed to make the economy viable.

It is probable that the most awful tyranny is the tyranny

of the crowd, for while imperial tyrants cause grievous harm, many of them at least keep the social structure operating; while the tyranny of the crowd is anti-leadership, and without leadership there is disorder—and no system can function for long in chaos.

## Unforeseen Consequences

As new forces arise to have an impact on how the whole system functions, they often have consequences that not only are unforeseen but that are opposite from what the instigators sought.

Of all the major revolutions, only the American Revolution resulted in its initiators having control of the new system and their principles being followed. That fact seems to be even more striking today, as evidenced by the consequences of revolutions in Russia, China, Southeast Asia, Fascist Italy, Nazi Germany, most of the former colonies, and the variety of repeated upheavals in Latin America, Africa, and elsewhere.

A major purpose of the black movement has been to gain for blacks greater stature, an expanded economic position, and a brighter future. But the massive expenditures in pursuing that objective and the weakening of all organizations' abilities to control their operations contributed to America's massive inflation and the resultant debilitated economy—which resulted in high unemployment and diminished growth of opportunities, both of which harm blacks more than any other segment of society.

Major goals of the female militants in America included making the society less violent and more orderly—to overcome what the activists saw as disorder that resulted from control by macho males. But among the consequences have been changes among men that have made many less assertive and less willing to assume initiative. It has had a marked effect on children, often making them feel less nurtured and more isolated. It has contributed to people's decreased willingness to follow the tenets of society, the authority of organizations and institutions, or the traditional rules.

It is characteristic of efforts to bring about change through force, rather than by persuasion, that unsought results ensue.

Until now, aggressive movements in America have been counterproductive, while the system has constantly renewed itself to accommodate causes that have won their cases through persuasion. Persuasion has been successful on behalf of women's rights, improved environment, noise abatement, greater attention to product safety, redesign of college enrollment and curricula, changes in elementary education, patients' rights, voting rights for blacks, and bringing the Vietnam War to an end. Violence has been unsuccessful on behalf of leftist revolution (the Symbianese Liberation Army, the Weathermen), black revolution (the Black Panthers and others), takeovers and vandalizing of college deans' offices and bombing of college research buildings.

But the cumulative weakening of organizations under pressures, and the multiplying of militant causes not only at home but around the world, make it uncertain that this failure of aggression will continue. Unless the leaders of all organizations and institutions learn to deal with the new climate of dissidence, and develop means to overcome it, they won't survive—and neither will the social system that the overwhelming majority of North Americans say they prefer to any other.

A society in which none of the organizations is able to function will go through convulsions. Out of the chaos would come an authority imposed by the strong and ruthless, abrogating all rules and restraints so it will be able to function. Once again, the result would be the opposite of that intended by the militants—and one that would hold nothing but despair for everyone.

We would revert to what has been the common structure of society at all other times and places.

At this time there is no need to despair. There are reasons to believe that we will come through this era and find a means to set our institutions onto their pilings again.

Samuel P. Huntington in *American Politics: The Politics of Disharmony* points out that we have gone through comparable spasms at sixty-year intervals: the Revolution, the Jacksonian era, the Progressive era, and the 1960s and their aftermath. Individuals in the earlier periods, too, leaped from cause to cause without seeing any of them through to a conclusion. The system bent, adjusted, absorbed such portions of the complaints as were sound, and went forward with its institutions in control. They learned to analyze the nature as well as the intent of the opposition, to assimilate the worthy aspects and confound the unworthy, and to follow the most vital of all instincts of humanity—the instinct for survival.

This is another time that requires such an adjustment. If the leadership of all organizations and institutions fails to understand what underlies the assaults on them, or fails to rally its intelligence and resources to meet the new threat, this brief success in operating a free society—with optimum benefits for all—may end. But the means to cope with the threat are known and available. They are the subject of the remaining chapters.

# CHAPTER 2

# What Caused the Shift

THE SWING OF PREDOMINANCE from leaders to various segments of the public has occurred in only a few years. No date can be cited for when the transition became evident, because there are many causes, each of which began to exert its influence at a different time.

There has probably never been a time when so many altering forces have been active at the same time. Any one of them would cause the social fabric to be transformed. All of them together pull that fabric in many directions simultaneously. And each of the forces works on all the others, modifying its nature and impact.

They are like many potent drugs taken into the body— each has its effect but together they have a synergistic effect that may negate the impact of any one and have a cumulative result that can be harmful or even fatal.

It is not possible merely to catalogue them and view

them in isolation. There is a complex pattern of developments that have had to be absorbed by human institutions—and there is no assurance that they have been absorbed without side effects that may leave the body of humanity wracked beyond redemption.

Together these forces add up to a new milieu in which events are determined not by powerful leaders or sanctified priests but by the human climate—the mass of attitudes among groups of people that determines how all institutions and organizations can function.

The human climate has become as important in determining how organizations can function as the natural climate is for the farmer.

This transformation is a phenomenon of the twentieth century—a century that long before its close has had three waves of drastic change in the major source of influence.

The first third of this century was shaped largely by science and invention. The technological and scientific reshaping of life had gained great momentum in the nineteenth century, but it was the sunburst of germinal developments between 1895 and World War II that closed gaps of time and distance, exploded people's ability to see and understand their world, made major inroads against disease, altered the understanding of the universe, penetrated the workings of the mind and psyche, and made possible man-made materials to meet thousands of needs.

In this period there came or reached technical feasibility the automobile, the airplane, the radio and television, the motion picture, the tractor, man-made drugs that defeated disease, air conditioning, plastics, insecticides, hybrid grains, atomic power, magnetic recording, the computer, space satellites, and the photocopier.

Great influences were being exerted by cultural, social, and other forces, but clearly that portion of the century was dominated by changes coming from science and invention.

The second segment of the century was dominated by organization and the rise of professional management. The inventors and scientists—Ford, Edison, Marconi, Fleming —were outpaced by the emergence of the huge and multi-faceted enterprises spawned by their work. The enterprises that grew up to develop and exploit their findings became far too vast and complicated for intuitive management. They gave way to people whose orientation and brain dominance inclined them toward running complex organizations, and who sought training to hone their talents.

The science of management budded, blossomed, and boomed. It created and embraced an array of sophisticated tools and techniques—coordinated and expanded by the computer and telecommunication. The great rewards were going (except for a few entertainers and athletes) to the managers of vast organizations, not to the creators of the new.

The science and techniques of management spread to all institutions. Governments called in professional managers to try to make sense of their labyrinth of functions, and then to create systems for carrying them out. The real work of Senators and Congressmen was being done by their staffs under the direction of administrative assistants trained to manage. Universities gave the mantle of the presidency to men and women who combined skill in managing their burgeoning institutions with the charm needed to win grants and raise funds. The position of hospital administrator became a position for someone trained for that task and not in medicine. The top military men became more and more those able to manage the vast system, rather than the Caesars, Hannibals, Napoleons, and Pattons who were masters of waging battles.

As always in the progression of human affairs, there has been a lag in recognizing what has been happening. It was some years after the managers took over from the inventors before people became aware that the innovator was no longer paramount. Now we have gone some years after the preeminence of the tough-minded administrator without recognizing that we are in a new era. For in this last third of the century, the world is being dominated by the human climate, in which what predominates are the attitudes of people and groups that try to express their urges.

## Wide Scope of Forces Behind Change

The array of forces behind this shift is long and varied. It ranges from the far reaches of the universe to the bedroom, from the highest levels of intellectual achievement to mass susceptibility to cults and fantasies.

● Most pervasive have been the spreading effects of technological and scientific development. They not only have themselves created a whole new spectrum of existence and perception, but they have made possible most of the other influences of change.

The effects of the technological revolution have been widely reported and need no detailing here. In total they have expanded the universe of human awareness, contact, and horizons as explosively as we now know the astronomical universe is expanding in all directions.

● Urbanization and suburbanization have changed not only the way hundreds of millions of people live, but also their outlook on what life has to offer. They have helped broaden people's expectations far beyond those of previous, mostly bucolic societies.

● Mass education and literacy have opened up hundreds of windows on the world, where before people tended to live in the narrow cells of their prejudices.

Education, even when flawed, opens the mind to new horizons and closes the darkness behind it.

Education also displays the great sunburst of what the world has to offer and holds out enough promise to arouse the person's demands. It promises to make each person it touches someone beyond the ordinary, with claims as well as rights, while leaving the fulfillment of the possibilities to what the person can personally achieve. So it has mass-produced dissidents the world over, who feel entitled to what seems to be promised but find most of what they seek beyond their reach.

• Electronic communication has come close to making the world Marshall McLuhan's Global Village, with people everywhere instantly aware of what before was out of mind because out of their sight or hearing.

The transistor radio has spread restlessness throughout the African jungles and the Southeast Asian rice fields. Television has projected into the daily life of much of the world its living though distorted view of what the world offers, and its terrors. It has broadened the stage of world attitudes more sharply than did the printing press, and in a far shorter time.

## Emergence of Self-Assertiveness

• As a result of many of the forces for change, we have been transformed from a world in which generations passed with almost no thought of one's status changing, to where almost everyone now believes that he or she counts and must have a voice in everything. This has reached its most advanced level in America where every person feels entitled to defy, block, harass, or sue to get his way, regardless of the consequences.

Illiterate parents immobilize schools intended to educate their children, because they want to make the judgments about how schools are run. Throughout the world, assertions are being made of the "right" of any individual to interfere in the functioning of every institution or organization.

• In 1960 a company making only fountain pens and pencils was known throughout the developed world as a major corporation. A firm with $500 million in annual sales was considered a giant. A hospital with 250 beds was a major medical center, and a bank with $1 billion in deposits was able to influence the world's financial events. The total United States budget was $76½ billion.

In the few years since, there has been exponential growth of the social and economic structure. The complexity of organizations has multiplied. That pen manufacturer's volume would be a small unit within any of a hundred corporations today. Many banks have made loans of more than $1 billion to single borrowers. The United States budget for fiscal year 1983 was $784 billion, plus a deficit of more than $100 billion.

• Resulting from this vast expansion, and making it possible, was a management revolution.

The inventors and innovators found their empires outgrowing the distinct traits that had bred their success. Their minds tended to be right-hemisphere dominated—attuned to seeing broad interrelationships, new concepts, creative approaches. The new need was for left-hemisphere dominance—disciplined adherence to measurables, resistance to what cannot be quantified.

The new scientific managers' skills were reflected in the language they used: the bottom line, tough-minded management, management by objectives, the payout, market share, return on investment, profit center, accountability, profit targets, earnings per share, cash flow—all quantifiable in numbers.

Where their predecessors had set their goals by their lifetime, and then a few years, the new milestone became a quarter of a year.

The professional manager was trained to concentrate on the measurable figures and to shun "fuzzy" matters that could not be processed with the computer. The computer and the professional manager surged into control of our institutions together, made for each other.

• Air travel and telecommunications not only tied various regions much closer together, as has often been noted;

they led to the mushrooming of hundreds of new metropolitan centers. Miami, Phoenix, Houston, San Diego, and many
others rose from obscurity in the United States. Remote cor-
ners such as Hong Kong and Singapore became new world
trade centers. Sao Paulo rose from a backwater to a jammed
metropolis of more than ten million people.

Dozens of smaller centers once limited to a day's driving
radius for their visitors got hooked into the networks of
long-distance telephone, network television, and jet airlines.

## Intellectuals' Hostility

• Along with the "new class" of professional managers
arose an almost opposite "new class" made up of what is
generically called intellectuals. They live with ideas and
words, and tend to be hostile to the practical-minded managers. They include college professors, writers, editors, artists,
social ideologues, government bureaucrats, creative people
in films and television.

They resent a world that puts higher store in running
our organizations and institutions than in their ideas and
language. They're sure they know best how all aspects of our
system should be run, while shunning as crass the function
of running them. To them, as Eric Hoffer pointed out, the
cornucopia of benefits for everyone represented by mid-
century America was not a blessing but a threat.

While professional managers ran the segments of society, intellectuals evolved and passed along to youth their opposing conception of what society should be.

• Among many contradictions was a strong denuncia-
tion by this intellectual elite of elitism. They were so determined to deny that *anything* can be measured that they insisted there was no difference between good and bad.

They advocated giving the same grades to the stupid and indolent as to the bright and conscientious lest the stupid have their psyches bruised. They labeled any community that maintained its cleanliness and low crime rates as *prima facie* bigoted. They plumped for the rights of criminals and ignored the rights of victims. They demanded that billions be poured into schooling for the uneducable but little for the gifted. They insisted that anyone having experience in any business should be disqualified from having any judgment over that business.

Mediocrity was glorified. Pass-fail was touted as the ideal grading system in schools. Unions disciplined workers who sought to do better or more than their indolent counterparts. Examinations to judge ability—particularly for teachers and other intellectuals—were fought ferociously.

• There has emerged a new view of the universe and humanity's place in it.

Knowledge of the vastness of the heavens and the likelihood that there are many other inhabited stars has further shrunk the individual's awe for institutions on earth. Far from seeming powerful and in control of events, institutions are seen as scarcely able to understand even minute aspects of the total order of things. The demotion of authority caused by the findings of Copernicus and Galileo has been acclerated along with the power of our telescopes.

• Along with the awesome advances of science in material things has come the assumption of scientific pretensions in social matters.

Theorists of how individuals, groups, politics, and money function assumed the label of "social scientists" as though what they deal with was subject to the same disciplines and assessments as science—even though few tenets in any of the fields have the agreement of its own practitioners.

On that basis they assume the right to tell all organizations and individuals how they should exist, though various economists, for instance, are always found on almost any side of any proposed course, and expert psychologists can be found in large numbers to testify for or against the mental stability of any person.

Like witch doctors, they insist on the validity of whatever point they choose, such as the need for law-abiding people to take murderers to their bosom, and castigate any points they dislike, such as processes for evaluation of various forms of intelligence.

● The combination of bloated expectations that all things can be provided, that all ills have a ready antidote, that science (even while creating new menaces) could come up with new miracles on order—these led to a whole society searching for easy answers.

Cults arose that promised simple routes to all of people's wishes—maximum pleasure now or selfless lining up for the next world; making humanity one huge body of mutual love or joining groups devoted to excluding all others.

In rapid order masses of people found their answers in zen, transactional analysis, pyschosynthesis, est, bioenergetics, scientology, energy flow, dance therapy, biofeedback, groping, sensitivity sessions, brass bracelets to fend off arthritis, Ankh emblems to propitiate the gods, charismatic religions, rolfing, Tufi, Tai Chi, pyramid power, pendulum power, Silva mind control, Satan worship, encounter therapy, primal scream, consciousness raising, talking to plants, ego states, stroking, transcendental meditation, the human potential movement.

While each of these arose and faded, their followers did not cease such searches for easy answers. Instead they continued to reject the stable organizations that made society function.

Stability offered no promises of miracles; orderly procedures could not fulfill promises overnight.

## Building of Unattainable Expectations

• The combination of many of these extensions of humanity's possibilities and the illusion that it can do everything for everybody—because "social scientists" have told us so—has spawned an almost universal sense of entitlement.

The fact that the totality of these expectations has always been unattainable, and that their constant expansion makes them ever more so, has been lost sight of.

Social engineers and governments everywhere contributed to building the expectations by funding their promises with inflated money. Yet even while this universal Ponzi scheme accelerated, dissatisfaction grew, because always what has been delivered is overlooked amidst the growing clamor for more.

Dissatisfaction with the institutions of society grew exactly while the greatest strides in history were made in the spread of education, improvement of general health, achievement of opportunity for hundreds of millions, goods and conveniences provided, comforts and luxuries afforded to most of the populace, availability and variety of recreation, availability of culture, and mental uplift.

With expectations held out at ever higher levels, the dissatisfactions led to self-fulfillment of the "promises"—the feeling that "I'll get mine" that has led to a contagion of rip-offs, cheating, fraud, and shoplifting; and outbursts of vandalism, aggression, and riots. Crime rates have shot up and tolerance of the crook has become part of the human climate cultivated by social engineers.

• The demand that everything be provided or made right created a litigious society.

Laws were passed by legislatures dominated by lawyers, and lawyers multiplied. Supply and demand prevailed—in this case, the supply of lawyers creating a demand for their services that encouraged everyone to "take it to court." One home owner who moved into the vicinity of an airport, knowing it was there, was able to tie up all improvements of that airport on the grounds that his right to quiet was being encroached.

Delay in the courts became a tactic that anyone could use on any issue; and the lawyers and judges welcomed the full string of appeals following any decision.

In 1982 the United States had one lawyer for every 383 people; Japan had one for every 10,781. And the morale of the Japanese people—as well as their productivity—was notably higher.

## Rejection of Sexual Restraints

● The sense of entitlement has spread from illogic of the mind to license for the genitals.

Abetted by development of the pill and propelled by a sense that everyone is entitled to whatever makes him or her feel good, the attitude has grown that the only limit on sexuality is stamina.

Antibiotics removed the penalties imposed by nature on promiscuity (until the emergence of resistant strains of gonococcus and herpes and the appearance of the deadly AIDS) and the new permissiveness of society removed the moral restraints.

Any authority of government, church, or even medicine over any form of copulation has become as outdated as the chaperon. Easy divorce and bypassing marriage have broken down the ethical restraint of concern for children's welfare; and other forms of sexual combinations have been classified as rights that no authority should have anything to say about.

● There have been reversals of many other "truths" that served as bulwarks of earlier authority.

There no longer is general agreement about the superiority of American society and systems, about the inevitability of progress, about the certainty that there will always be an underclass, that extra effort and extra contribution to humanity should be rewarded.

• The nature of military power has been transformed.

The nuclear bomb created a mushroom cloud of people's alarm over their inability to escape from or survive the ultimate war. It created two "master powers" who at the same time became impotent in waging wars in Southeast Asia and Afghanistan.

Primitive bands demonstrated their ability to confound massive forces.

Power by terror became simultaneously more awful and less real.

• The struggle against the Vietnam War became a dramatic demonstration of how the supposedly powerless could hamstring the supposedly powerful leadership of the world's No. 1 nation. It became both a classroom in opposition to authority and a promise of what could be done in other revolts.

The Vietnam protests taught millions of people how to disrupt, how to form coalitions, how to seduce the media.

It greatly accelerated the "democratization" of the armed forces, which removed the authority of officers to demand action. That brought into question whether all the vast armaments America possessed really represented any effective power at all.

As a consequence of these and other pressures of change, the institutions that make up society came under siege.


## Proliferation of Causes

A partial list of "issues" on which various organizations and institutions have been attacked shows how the spirit of revolt permeates the system:

Abortion
Anti-abortion
School prayer
Housing
Crime
Abuse of spouses
Forced promotion by class
Demand for roads
Police brutality
Discrimination in housing
Sex education
Access to everything for the
 handicapped
Opposition to tests and
 evaluation
Strip mining
Forced school busing
Representation of the un-
 educated on school boards
Job training
Family planning
Fire protection
Taxes
Opposition to sex education
Free legal services
Consumer rights
Treaty rights
Bilingual education
Tenants' rights
Lower rents
Day care services
Transportation
Sexual harassment

Infant formula
Easy access to credit
Occupational health
Occupational safety
Political representation
Anti-nuclear energy
Lower phone bills
Drug abuse
Harassment of drug users
Free college education
Protection of wilderness
Water pollution
Air pollution
Waste disposal
Nuclear energy
Unemployment
Bigger welfare checks
Free recreation facilities
Red-lining
Free health care
Rat control
Schools
Access to services
Child abuse
Lower utility bills
Opposition to cutoffs or evic-
 tion for nonpayment
Opposition to enforcing im-
 migration laws
Telephone bills
Censorship of books, TV,
 films
Opposition to roads

The constant barrage of attacks on authority has created
a climate in which, as Daniel Yankelovich put it:

Authority itself has become suspect. This attitude shows
up in public-opinion surveys in the form of lower confidence scores for all institutions—government, business,
the professions, the courts, the colleges, the press. . . . It
shows up in the form of increasing crime and violence,

and growing disrespect for our system of criminal justice. And now it is starting to show up in tolerance for guile and subterfuge . . ."[1]

What began with a new distrust of leaders is becoming almost universal distrust of everyone. That is the brink of universal paranoia. Leaders of our organizations and institutions need to understand what underlies this malaise and how to overcome it.

The time seems to be right. Uneasiness about this deterioration of leadership is shown in a Gallup poll (December, 1981): 94 percent of the public said they would welcome more respect for authority.

---

[1] "Lying Well Is the Best Revenge," *Psychology Today*, August, 1982.

# SECTION TWO

# Understanding What's Behind the Problem

# CHAPTER 3

# Behind the Attitudes of Leaders

THE SWITCH FROM POWER centered in organizations and institutions to power focused among various groups of people has transformed the requirements for leadership of organizations.

The managerial revolution bred a distinct type of leader. Running complex organizations requires the skills of disciplined people who can cut through masses of varied information and get to the facts so they can reach informed judgments. Their need created "the knowledge revolution" and absorbed it.

The great development of industry, health care, research, education, government, universities, the armed forces, foundations, and all other fields was made possible by emergence of such masterly managers. They are pre-selected, bred, and advanced on the basis of their concentration on the hard-fact approach.

Young people with typical left-brain dominance—strong orientation to specific facts, numbers, linear relationships—are attracted to education for management, while those who tend to see broad patterns and infinite interrelationships tend to be repelled by that type of career. Thus, the future masterly manager is pre-selected by his or her inherent inclinations.

Education then burnishes the person's inclinations and points him/her to a graduate school of business. There he is surrounded by others with precisely the same inclinations, interests, and way of seeing things. Grades reflect how well the person excels in what tangible-minded teachers provide. Until recently the revered cornerstone of the MBA programs was the case method—which stresses past situations and grades students on their measurable responses.

Once out of school and launched on a career path, the manager again is surrounded by like-minded people and evaluated on the basis of *measurements*—expressed in various forms of counting. Dossiers are filled with evaluation reports that employ detailed forms calling for specific ratings. The intelligent young manager, if he was not already inclined to focus only on what can be measured, soon learns to give attention only to what will add to the score in the dossier.

The greatest strength of the masterly manager is discipline of mind. He or she focuses on the facts and the realities, not letting loose ends or fuzzy sentiments take the eye off the solid goal. He abhors things that interfere with measurability, predictability, and accountability. His precise mind made necessary the computer, which reasons through the use of numbers; and the numbers of the computer become the touchstone of reality. In this logic, if it can't be tabulated, "it doesn't add up" and so is given little attention.

However, the requirements of the sophisticated organization are being changed by precisely the imprecise elements that can't be counted, plotted, or tracked—the attitudes of people. Public attitudes are causing managers of all kinds of organizations and institutions their greatest troubles: ethnic pride, environmentalism, conservation, religious fervor, the demands of entitlement, minority demands, women's claims, union policies, community positions, opposition to bigness, international ferments, demand for individual choice.

The masterly manager is trained to *maximize certainty* by focusing on forms, reports, charts, balance sheets, formulas, readouts, and accountability statements. The world in which the organization must function is marked by constant upsets, impacts, and *uncertainties.*

It is as though one trained four years to compete in the Olympic shotput and then was entered in gymnastics.

The manager was trained to master the elements that make up the *internal* organization and its functions (see Figure 3-1).

The new pattern of *external* forces based on group attitudes presents an opposite picture (Figure 3-2).

## Reasons for Resistance

An uneasy awakening began when it became evident that the old pattern was meeting resistance. It used to be that management consisted of (1) tough-minded concentration on "facts" (one of the most widely read books of its era was

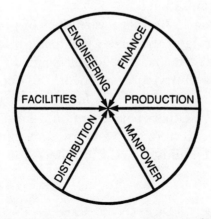

**Figure 3-1. Focus of Internal-Oriented Manager**

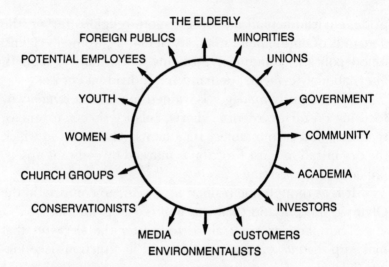

**Figure 3-2. Focus of Manager in New Human Climate**

titled *Tough-Minded Management*[1]); and (2) directing others to carry out management's decisions.

Some sensitive observers broached recognition of "the people factor." But even the most influential of them, such as Douglas McGregor, sought only to fine-tune the masterly manager's approach, not to shift it. McGregor's X and Y Theory—propounding that decision-making proceed from group considerations rather than as dictatorial edicts from above—assumed that all decisions would still be controlled *within* the organization.

During the 1970s there were signs of growing recognition that the role of the leader was being transformed.

Foresighted managers such as Reginald Jones of General Electric and Irving Shapiro of DuPont revealed that their main focal points were the forces generated by external public attitudes. Others paid attention. Glimmers of this recognition appeared faintly among university presidents, health center administrators, and others. But it is still of low candlepower.

---

[1]Now in Third Edition. By J.D. Batten. American Management Association. 1978.

Even the widely read book, *In Search of Excellence*, which stresses the need for managers to broaden their viewpoints and develop sensitivity to people, makes no mention of any *external* groups except customers.

There are a number of reasons why the shifting of gears has been slow and marked by grinding resistance:

- The demands were new and unexpected. Everyone is disoriented by phenomena that aren't supposed to occur—especially men and women who have achieved status and prosperity by following a course opposite to what is now emerging. The new demands appear as a direct affront to the leader's sense of worthiness.

- The new demands are outside of the organization. All their adult lives, leaders have been focusing on getting ahead within their organizations. They are masters at working the organization as well as at what they are skilled in doing. External forces are "externalities"— outside nuisances—until they gum up the machinery.

- They are opposite to the standards of the disciplined mind, which expects everything to have its place and to perform, like a scientific process, as it's supposed to perform. They are exactly the "fuzzy minded" considerations that he has been warned to ignore throughout his training and apprenticeship.

- They call for sharing his hard-earned power and catering to those whom he has risen above in the competition for success and stature. He is faced with abrogating the axiom that no one ever willingly gives up a position of power, except to gain power in other forms.

- They add several stages to the process of reaching decisions, and then to the process of getting things done. It's not "efficient." It is contrary to the masterly manager's "do it now" personality that earned him his advanced stature.

- At the same time that they slow things up, they are propelled by instant widespread communication. The old privilege of reaching decisions after studied consideration is shattered. Control over the sequence of decision-making, planning, assignment, and execution is shaken. Now, instant communication, most of it beyond the manager's control, creates instant demand for responses. It severely penalizes any appearance of uncertainty while responding to demands for immediate answers and solutions. It greatly speeds up the time for making many decisions—and then distorts the careful process of putting all the pieces into place and developing a precise timetable. It tends to change decision-making from studied judgment to "shooting from the hip."

- Leaders are the winners in the human competition. Winners are busy. They have empires they feel are looking to them for leadership. They have responsibilities that weigh on them and that call for responsible actions. But those people they consider to be the losers have lots of time and energy—and now they probably are funded with resources squeezed out of the winners to be used against them, in the form of assured income, ready access to lawyers and the courts, and a government bureaucracy favoring the "little man."

## Openness to New Approaches

The conditions behind the attitudes of leaders include one important trait that is both a danger and an advantage. As Eric Hoffer pointed out in *The True Believer*:

The self-confidence of even the consistently successful is never absolute. They are never sure that they know all the ingredients which go into the making of their success. The outside world seems to them a precariously balanced mechanism, and so long as it ticks in their favor they are afraid to tinker with it.

Leaders sense that the stability that holds things together is something of a miracle—that keeping millions of diverse elements in some kind of equilibrium is too sensitive a phenomenon to endanger with untried processes. That is what makes leaders "conservative," even while they are dedicated to bringing about *their* changes through the success of their efforts.

Yet it is also an advantage and the main source of assurance that the system will adjust and go on with new forms of stability. Uncertainty that they're right opens leaders' minds—when signs of alarm become clear. They become receptive to new counsel. They become ready to bring to their aid the people who can read the dynamics of the new climate, help overcome the leaders' blind spots, help plot the strategies, and devise programs that will meet the challenges.

Because mankind is the most adaptable of all species, the social systems created by mankind are adaptable, over a period of time. It's probable that today's society will also adapt when the needs are made clear, the challenges are evident, and the means of meeting them are understood.

# CHAPTER 4

# Types of Opponents

COLUMBUS SET OUT FOR CHINA without knowing what lay in his course, but in the 500 years since then decision-makers have gradually learned to find out in advance what they'll be dealing with.

Politicians spend much of their campaign budget doing research among the voters. Corporations size up the market before venturing a new product. They carefully assess the mood and motivations of their employees. Investment bankers earn millions in fees for their ability to size up what investors will be willing to pay for a new security.

Yet when it comes to dealing with opposition groups, even sophisticated leaders proceed without a compass or a survey. They wouldn't drive ten miles in an unknown area without a map, but they gamble the survival of their organizations on their blind feelings about their adversaries.

Failing to apply the time and perception needed to understand the nature and motivation of opposing groups is probably the greatest neglect of leaders.

They became leaders because they have a built-in feeling for how organizations function. By definition, a leader is a specialist in leading a group or an organization. Accordingly, the existence of people who don't want the organization to fulfill its purposes is seen as an aberration—a freak of nature akin to a rogue elephant or a celibate in a harem.

Actually, of course, history is mostly a chronicle of the efforts of leaders to hold their power, or extend it, in the face of masses who depended on them but resented their powers. Dissent is not an aberration but the norm.

Existence of insurgents against leadership not only is not new, it is built into the human psyche. It is not a nuisance that will go away "when things return to normal" or "when we get over this crazy period we're in."

So the starting point for overcoming opposition is to recognize the depths of its roots, and then to understand the nature and motivations of opponents.

A common mistake is assuming that all those who oppose an institution are alike and should be dealt with in the same way. That comes from the penchant for classifying things and putting labels on them. That is an error in dealing with diverse humanity, since each person is unique. Sizing up one is difficult; categorizing large numbers of them is folly.

Actually, there are several ways in which opponents fall into a wide range of classifications. Probably the most important is their motivations, which spring from many different causes.

Following are five main classifications based on the *personality* of those included. Personality involved with any specific cause (which may be different from the same person's personality on all other matters) determines (1) the reason for holding the opinion involved; (2) the approach likely to be taken in expressing that opinion; (3) the kind of group the person is likely to ally with; (4) how the person will respond to various arguments or persuasion; (5) how he or she will respond to opposition or intransigence; (6) and what he or she is likely to do after the question involved is past.

In general, for the sake of understanding, opponents can be grouped into at least five classifications of personality:

1. *Advocates.* These are people who propose something they believe in, such as a reduction in emissions of carbon dioxide. Leaders often are advocates, such as when a businessman proposes that lower taxes would help the economy and increase employment. An advocate may propose that a company's building be named an historical monument because she thinks it's beautiful and it would be a shame to raze it.

2. *Dissidents.* They are against something—and sometimes are against many things because it is their character to be sour on things as they are. A dissident may only oppose hiring practices involving women, or be against most things done by most organizations.

3. *Activists.* They want to get something done or something changed. Their instinct is, "Don't just stand in the picket line—do something!" They may want to push legislation through Congress, stop construction of a new highway, or pass an amendment forbidding abortion.

4. *Zealots.* They may have some traits of the others, but they are distinguished by an overriding singlemindedness. They are likely to be absorbed with one issue—such as stopping construction of power plants or forcing the "liberation" of some region—and are likely to feel that their mission in life is to achieve that purpose by aggressive means.

5. *Fanatics.* They are zealots with their stabilizers removed. They kill innocent people with bombs or machine guns. They hijack airplanes and terrorize hostages. They may blackmail a country with nuclear bombs.

Fanatical terrorists are a problem outside the scope of other considerations. Protection against their onslaughts and the forceful means to extirpate them call for the full power of established police and military authority.

Dealing with the other four types requires being sensitive to the psyche of the people involved.

Clearly, the means used to deal with an advocate will be futile with a zealot. Logic, persuasion, seeking agreements based on mutual compromise—all of these are based on a reasonable desire to resolve the matter and go on with other things. To the zealot there are no other things; his issue is the predominant matter in life. To resolve it on any basis but absolute surrender by the organization is unthinkable.

On the other hand, to treat an advocate in the same way one treats a zealot results in creating hatred where none existed. The sight of police dogs attacking passive supporters of blacks marching in Alabama shook millions of Americans out of their apathy about extending voting by blacks.

The basis for dealing with reasonable people is reason.

It is useless to try to reason with zealots or revolutionaries. By definition, they are immune to reason. They cannot be dissuaded by direct persuasion, no matter how sound.

The way to overcome zealots is to wither away the support they depend on.

Every group needs the material and psychological support of others—constituents, parishioners, media, the public. When constituents cool in their support, the small band of zealots is isolated and its momentum wanes. Even the most successful and powerful group of zealots in modern history—the Nazis in Germany—were unable to continue when the support of the populace drained away.

Accordingly, efforts should not be directed at trying to convert the zealots but should be aimed at weakening the unthinking support that others have been giving to these opponents.

The differences between these personalities account for

much of the splintering that goes on constantly in various movements. Zealots and activists become impatient with the impassionate approach of advocates and break away. Then the zealots tend to find the activists are not "dedicated" enough because they may have concern for other issues or for the consequences of their actions.

Zealots, especially, are egocentric. They find it difficult to sit in an audience; they must run the show. They tend to find others with more moderate approaches to be enemies: "If you're not for me, you're against me." They are like the Stalinists who came to hate other Communists more than their original common enemies.

Reason can be used, in proper form, to deal with advocates; logic and selected emotions with dissidents; logic and strategic actions with activists. But you cannot change a zealot by any direct approach. Logic and reason will probably be met by fury, as being devious efforts to escape the one "true answer" that the zealot espouses. You cannot ignore the zealot, as you might some of the others for a time. Coping with the zealot calls for creating a climate of opinion and understanding among the public around him. That will isolate the zealot and wither his zeal. The zealots of the '60s who tried to destroy society's foundations were not converted by persuasion; they lost the base of public support and were left to shrivel into impotence.

Even within these categories there must be left a margin for overlap. And even more important is the volatility of individuals.

A common trait of people who are attracted to causes is their changeability. Former Communists often make the most vocal Fascists. Former divinity students become atheists, and there is no more devout singer of hymns and hosannas than the former nonbeliever.

Women who were singleminded nurturers of families have become zealots of women's liberation, such as Betty Friedan—and many a former "libber" now cherishes her hearth and children. Throughout history former libertines have become the most repressive foes of sexual liberty.

Every assessment of the makeup, nature, source, and probable course of opponents must avoid the kind of pigeonholed identification and fixed description that is the natural penchant of the organized mind.

## Roots of Opposition

Another process for understanding opposition groups is studying the basis for their makeup. Opposition groups are not random assemblies any more than are universities, businesses, armies, or congregations.

When the genesis of the group can be understood on the basis of what brought it together *besides the issue in question*, you are a long way toward knowing how to deal with it.

Constituencies of opposition movements often have one predominant root. It may be race, such as civil rights groups. It may be language, such as advocates of bilingual education. It may be religion, such as anti-abortion groups. It may be a common hand in others' pockets, such as recipients of a given government handout.

What brings opponents together may be predominantly location, such as a given community or parents with children in a specific school. Location may be the focus for a group, such as Iranian students in the United States. But location and national heritage may not be enough to label them. Some Iranian students are activists for the mullah government and others are activists against it. Identification of a group is seldom simple.

Another identification that can mislead is ideology. People marching against a nuclear power plant will include not only those concerned with safety but those who see a chance to cripple the economic system and make it easier prey for socialism.

To understand opponents and think clearly about dealing with them requires a penetrating understanding of where they come from.

Growth of the number of activist protesters and the number of causes they espouse is now built into our system.

Millions of people have been educated to think they should have a special role in our society. Colleges proffer degrees as freedom from routine roles and marks of leadership (even while they propound "equality" for everyone).

Only a few find they can attain dreamed-of influence. The world won't bow to their wisdom. Disillusion sets in.

As Eric Hoffer said: "There is nothing more explosive than a skilled population condemned to inaction." The problem is most acute among those educated faster than they can be absorbed: blacks, many women, and social-science majors.

Those led to expect great things seek to justify themselves. They're disappointed with their small roles; so they have the time, the inclination, and the opportunity to attack the structure. The increased leisure and affluence of the system they attack makes constant activism possible.

But no system will ever absorb a near-majority of people expecting to be leaders; so we are developing a whole society of bored and frustrated people. They will spend their time trying to force change . . . and when change comes, it will suit only a few, so most will be constantly pressing for other changes.

## The Importance of Disaffection

While on most issues many of the opponents are clear-thinking and reasonable, there is also a large number who are not.

Ironically, they are products of the progress that has been made in almost all aspects of society during their lifetime. So many problems have been alleviated into near invisibility that these people now have become perfectionists.

If there is a sign that something is short of perfect, they feel it must be condemned. They consider it reasonable to demand 100 percent purity of all waterways (which nature has never achieved); pollution levels for cars beyond practical technology (while they drive their own polluting cars to protest rallies); and regulations for product safety that would outlaw the match if it were introduced today (while in their work they resent efforts to raise standards of performance).

They epitomize a new psychological syndrome that can be expressed: "*You* have to be coerced; let *me* alone."

They not only want perfect conditions but they want them to come easily. In politics, economics, crime, environment, and every other problem that has faced humanity since prehistory, they expect "quick fixes." That accounts for the endless grasping we have seen of creeds, cults, fads, and fetishes.

The easy answer, however, comes to them most probably from outside established authority. Reports in the popular press of miracle cures speed through the populace; cautious studies about cures that may prove solid in a few years, after careful testing, are all but ignored.

Ideas are accepted today, among such people, in inverse ratio to the ideas' identification with centers of authority. They are most likely to catch on (for a while) if they come from somewhere within the populace itself—or seem to.

As we shall see in Chapter 20, the inherent nature of most opponents—what makes them lash out at organizations and institutions—provides the key to preventing their disruption of orderly systems.

# CHAPTER 5

# How Opponents Operate

OPPOSITION USUALLY TAKES ONE OF THREE FORMS:

*1. A grievance or request expressed by various people in an unorganized way.*

A company may hear separately from a number of families nearby about the noise caused by workers starting to operate outside machinery at 7 a.m. At that stage, a review of the grievance and finding a solution—such as negotiating with the union to delay the early starting time desired by workers who want to quit at 3 p.m. so they can go fishing—can overcome the opposition with little difficulty.

Most opposition encountered by organizations is this unorganized type and usually can be resolved with little upset or cost. In other cases, effective negotiating techniques can bring about a compromise that also will forestall trouble.

*2. A simple request or complaint from a group such as neighbors concerned about a planned waste disposal system.*

48

The people involved have not been critics in the past and have only this one concern. Dealing with this sort of opposition is treated in the next chapter.

These two types of opposition are familiar. Their importance here is primarily to make certain that when the organization encounters opposition it consider first whether it is this type of simple appeal. Any criticism or signs of disaffection should be taken seriously, but it would be a mistake to respond to them as if they were systematic, organized confrontations.

3. *Organized activist pressure on the organization from a group or a composite of groups.*

Usually it is easy to tell when the opposition is of this type. A group that has assumed a name—such as Valley Park Citizens Against Noise Pollution—has gone beyond the stage of transient criticism. If stories appear in the newspapers or on TV accusing the organization of something, there is probably an activist group behind them. If any kind of systematic pressures are experienced—a letter-writing campaign, picketing, threats of boycotts, and so on—there is clearly an activist movement involved.

Encountering an activist movement should not be a surprise most of the time, if the organization has been alert to the signals we've mentioned: reviewing complaints, tracking letters received, watching the media that report on various outside interests, maintaining communication lines with employees at all levels, encouraging church leaders and others close to the people to report what's being discussed.

Whether the emergence of the activist group is predicted or a surprise, however, it's vital to start with an objective and dispassionate understanding of the nature, goals, and problems of the group.

Almost all activist groups must be effective on three fronts at one time:

  1. They must direct their efforts at getting responsive change from the organization that is its target.

2. They must gain the active support or at least the sympathy of the public it seeks to sway—the general public, a specific government agency, members of a body such as a firm's customers or a hospital's patients.

3. They must win, hold, enthuse, and motivate their own supporters. For every group, *that is a struggle*.

Heads of targeted organizations tend to consider the groups that confront them as cohesive, emotionalized, dedicated phalanxes. Actually, these groups are beset by the volatility and diverse motives of their supporters. As we shall see in Chapter 15, the very traits that make people susceptible to aligning with an activist group make them susceptible to breaking away.

It is important here to contemplate what Saul Alinsky said was one of the first rules of activism: Power is not only what you have but what the enemy thinks you have. Organization leaders who attribute more cohesion and steadfastness to their opponents than really exist tend to give their opponents strength they do not have.

The heads of organizations, when confronted with an activist threat, tend to think first about themselves as targets. Then they may consider the publics that the group is aiming its appeals at. They seldom recognize the importance of the activists' internal stresses. Yet those may be most important in determining the outcome.

## Priorities of Activist Groups

The activist group has three simultaneous priorities:

- Its own support;
- The public it's wooing (usually via the media);
- The decision-making arena (legislative body, regulatory agency, court).

Often, in a fourth priority, is the targeted organization itself. In many cases, however, the objective is not to grapple with the targeted organization but only to use it as a foil for "demonstrating" the merits of the group's case. That is the situation, for instance, when the issue is industrial waste disposal, clean air, noise at an airport, parking of students near a college, and many other issues. The organization is targeted not so much to get it to change its practices as to focus on a perpetrator that a legislature, regulatory agency, or court should require to change.

One of the most common errors made by organizations is to respond to activists' initiatives in defense of themselves rather than to be authoritative parties in consideration of the problem.

It is the activists' need to influence all three of its priority publics that so often leads to their playing to the grandstand. The grandstand—where there can be an open field view of the action—is where the group's hoped-for supporters are, where the media can be lured into reporting the fray, and where decision-makers among legislators and government employees can be led to believe they are observing the public's interest.

Here, as in many other aspects of activism, the act that is put on overshadows the reality. In this age of TV drama and superficiality, that "act" can often displace reality. Facts, "acts," and "factoids"—supposed facts made out of partial truths, wishful assertions, vindictive claims, or imagined musings—all get mixed together on the public agenda. It is hard for fact-minded managers and leaders to accept, but facts have no greater likelihood of winning out than factoids or acts—unless masterly planning and strategy are applied throughout the process.

## Knowing the Opponents

Things that must be known about the opponents include:

1. Transient dissatisfactions don't form into an activist movement until they are shaped by an organizer or agitator.

The Bolsheviks in Russia were a desperate rabble until the master organizer, Lenin, rose as their leader. Alinsky not only shaped the role of the non-violent agitator but wrote the books that have guided thousands of others.

One of the most important steps for any organization concerned about becoming a target is to identify and study carefully those who might be able to agitate the nebulous individuals into a group.

In a study of 157 leaders of major "public-interest" groups, S. Robert Lichter of George Washington University and Stanley Rothman of Smith College found that 90 percent call themselves leftists, 8 percent middle-of-the-roaders and only 2 percent right of center. Only 2 percent voted for Reagan in 1980, 3 percent for Ford in 1976.

Ninety-four percent believe that government should redistribute income. In rating the greatest influences in society, they list business first, followed by the media, the military, government agencies, and unions. They think the order of power *should* be: consumer groups, blacks, intellectuals, feminists, unions—with business in eighth place.

2. People who join movements—aside from direct personal concerns such as the water they drink and the safety of their children—tend to be restive or bored with their lives. The movement meets a need *besides the purpose it espouses.* And it can lose their support to another movement or anything else that promises relief from restiveness or boredom.

3. People who form movements usually have an innate sense of being the weak—the imposed upon. They need to bolster their resolve by recruiting respected supporters—churchmen, educators, artists. These happen also to be estranged from most other organizations, because they are not dominant in a world that rewards practical achievements.

4. Most people who join activist movements see everything in black-or-white terms. That simplistic frame of mind seeks immediate and clear-cut solutions to problems that are immediately visible. They block out information that may complicate their viewpoint and they tend to ignore long-term

consequences. Some people who marched to boost the wages of illegal aliens working in the vegetable fields of California later picketed supermarkets when the prices of vegetables went up. Some people who demonstrated for boosting government welfare programs also joined groups protesting inflation-boosted prices and later were in the forefront of protesters against budget cuts that lowered inflated prices.

5. People form into groups when they believe they have the power to change a situation. If they don't have that belief, they don't think about it. So a movement combines in its members a sense of having some power and a sense that the chosen target is vulnerable. They may try to close down a manufacturing plant but not an armed military camp. They may demonstrate outside a church marked for closing, but won't storm the cardinal's cathedral.

6. People who form into movements have free time and energy—and often available assets to pay their own costs. One of the major reasons for the great increase in activism in this generation is the great decrease in the time required to earn a living or an education. People who work seven hours a day, five days a week, with three to fourteen weeks of vacation have both time and energy that they can seek outlets for.

7. Movements live on enthusiasm—which is hard to maintain amid doubts. Alinsky's instruction to organizers was to paint their cause always as 100 percent pure and the opponents' always as 100 percent evil. "You do what you can with what you have and clothe it with moral garments," he said.

The liberal *New York Times Magazine* acknowledges:

> There is no pretense of objectivity in these briefings (of the Illinois Public Action Council). In the Populist tradition, the issue is black and white: the people versus big business and government.

8. The purpose of a movement is to bring about change. All change means disorganizing what exists and or-

ganizing something new. So the first thrust of a movement is toward disorganization—upsetting whatever is the target to assuage what the members are upset about.

9. The movement's organizer must stay within the experience of his people. Sprightly ladies from Winnetka may chant to disrupt an organization's meeting but they are not likely to throw rotten eggs at a university president.

10. The movement, having to grab the public attention, must make itself visible. At the same time, it must not lose its role as the underdog by making the target into a put-upon martyr. Picketing has lost its effectiveness because it became so common it lost its ability to gain attention. Bombs created sympathy even for the Chase Manhattan Bank during the furor over ousting the Shah of Iran.

11. Movements thrive on the sensitivity of powerful organizations to unfavorable attention. "Communication—which includes the concept of corporate image and political programs—is the flywheel of American society; bend it, and you can cause the entire machine to shudder and belch," said Charles McCarry in *Citizen Nader*.

12. Activists, feeling that they alone are in the right and also feeling deprived because they have little money of their own, consider it balancing the scales to make their opponents pay for all actions. They feel that neither the costs nor the consequences of their acts should be their responsibility. If they go to court, they expect taxpayers to pay for their legal fees and the costs of the courts, while any awards they receive will be theirs. If a city is closed down or a company incurs huge losses because of activist action, the taxpayers and the stockholders must bear the expense.

13. Believing that they have 100 percent right on their side, many activists consider any tactics permissible to them. In fact, Alinsky taught that the penchant of organizations to act by rules of fair conduct was a weakness that activists should exploit. By assuming a holy mantle—religious or otherwise—some activists consider duplicity or even treachery one of their tools. Even in lesser forms, this at-

titude shows up in negotiations as a one-sided approach to morality.

After negotiating with church-related groups for more than two years to work out a code for distributing infant formula in poor countries, and believing they had a workable agreement, the formula producers were confronted with a non-negotiable demand that they accept a different code— one they could not follow. The activists who claimed they spoke for church people—and therefore for God—defended their tactics on the basis that since what they wanted was desired by agents of God they were justified in following such practices.

14. The most common strategy is to start in a small way, gain some concessions so victories can be demonstrated, rally support and build up membership, and—not settling for the concessions—escalate the demands. Groups may start with a campaign of letters, petitions, and negotiating sessions. Whatever is gained is used to feed the group's momentum. And any partial victory is hailed as a triumph. ". . . to the organizer, compromise is a key and beautiful word," Alinsky said. "If you start with nothing, demand 100 percent, then compromise for 30 percent, you're 30 percent ahead."

After gains from the mild and predictably successful tactics, the strategy is to move up to tougher demands with such techniques as sit-ins, boycotts, and disruptions.

15. Sophisticated organizers know that in dealing with a sophisticated opponent there can be no negotiation unless they have the power to compel negotiation. As managers come to recognize that making concessions on early demands does not usually end a group's pressures, activists have learned to maximize their negotiating power at each stage. Their strategy is to maintain and increase pressure, confident that the opposition will finally give in so it can focus on its essential functions or end the whiplash on attitudes of its constituents.

16. Activist groups do not fade away when they have won some gains—even those that may have been its first

objectives. They usually go on to more and more demands until they have achieved capitulation or their efforts cease to bring enough results to keep their members steamed up.

It is clear from a review of these facts that leaders of target organizations must apply discerning judgment at many stages. It is vital not to underestimate the situation at any juncture. But in various situations, overreacting to the seriousness of opposition can be as harmful as apathy.

For instance, every organization frequently encounters requests, suggestions, complaints, and other expressions that represent legitimate interests. To deal with these as though they were activist attacks is more damaging than grappling with an activist group and having to make concessions. In the next chapter we will look at the treatment of such legitimate interests.

# CHAPTER 6

# Dealing with Opponents' Legitimate Interests

THOUGH NO ONE LIKES TO HAVE OTHERS OPPOSE HIS OR HER INTERESTS, that aversion is naturally greatest among leaders. They have the stressful responsibility for balancing diverse factors to enable their organizations to function; they are averse to having other factors added, especially those that would pull them in directions opposite to where they seek to go. They have risen because they demonstrated knowledge of what the organization can do and needs; they see outsiders' demands as ignorant interference. And because they grow accustomed to having others accept their wisdom and authority, their reaction to contradiction and opposition is affected by emotion.

Yet every organization will always have outsiders who criticize it. In fact, probably nothing is so certain to cause an organization's dissolution as closing out the less-than-worshipful inputs of intelligent outsiders.

The Nixon White House demonstrated how deluded and even deranged a closed atmosphere can make the most powerful office. Many large corporations that are struggling through the '80s listened only to their own circle of like-minded executives in the '70s.

That syndrome was explained in 1979 by Dr. David G. Myers, a noted expert on intergroup relations:

> . . . like-minded people increasingly associate with each other as a conflict evolves, amplifying their shared tendencies. . . . Discussion generally strengthens the average inclination held by group members before the discussion.[1]

Competition is necessary for any person or organization to function at optimum level. Competition of ideas is a stimulus of judgment and a monitor of effectiveness.

Accordingly, a basic rule in assessing opponents is: Allow room for normal expression of opinions and criticisms; provide for free interchange. The role of the individual and groups of individuals is now a reality. Only emergence of a Fascist-like repression—which would require the acquiescence of most of the people who now are anti-restraint—could stifle them.

If exchange of opinion and suggestions is free, and if the tone is kept unheated so logic can prevail, the best of combined thinking is likely to prevail in the long run.

Another rule is: Listen—they may have something to offer. The combination of widespread education and freedom to express oneself has made millions of people capable of making worthwhile suggestions—even if they start as criticisms.

Thousands of changes adopted by large organizations have come from non-professionals on the outside. Most of the myriad uses for Scotch tape, for example, were de-

---

[1]"How Groups Identify Decisions," *Human Nature*, March 1979, pp. 34-9.

veloped by buyers who tried it for purposes the manufacturer never envisioned. Many a product improvement has resulted from listening to a dissatisfied customer. Successful politicians go back to their districts periodically to hear from the voters—not just to ask their supporters for their votes.

A third rule: If a group has legitimate arguments and shows it has a sound approach, enlist its leaders. Often they will make great contributions as employees. They might be retained as consultants. Or they may become active in a new working group you set up jointly.

Much of the opposition to established systems results from old practices that shut out many of the most fertile groups from participation in those systems. In every society, those in the ruling groups educate outsiders but tend to bar the way upward in the "establishment" organizations. In the United States the result was that hundreds of thousands of aggressive, assertive young people—barred from major corporations and banks—moved into the fields open to them: the media, union organizing, academia, school teaching, activism, social work. Those became the very fields that spawned the virulent anti-establishment movements that arose after World War II.

But that pattern has changed. It has been largely the children of those who gained acceptance, as well as offspring of established families, who led the revolt over Vietnam. Once their spirit of revolt was honed, they joined the small group of activists for other causes—such as blacks' demands and migrant farm workers—to spawn activism for the many causes we've mentioned. They took for granted the gains their parents had wrenched from a tough world. Those no longer presented a challenge. With all the needs of their lives assured, their expectations were jaded; so they were ripe for being lured by the new challenges they saw.

They followed an old tradition: the children of powerful families sought causes that attacked evident power. In the 1850s the scions of New England aristocrats attacked the aristocrats of the South who owned slaves. In the early 1900s

they attacked the evils of alcohol—other people's pleasure—
to promote Prohibition. In the 1930s they were among the
most vocal of the early New Dealers. Always they seek to
impose their "superior morality" on those too benighted to
see their visions.

## Need for Objective Judgment

An important point is that many causes have merit—but
that the leaders of the organization being attacked may be
least able to see it. It is precisely when outside pressures are
building against the practices of an organization that it most
needs the thinking of intelligent outside people.

During 1981, when many corporations were trying to
get regulations on environmentalism loosened, the Sierra
Club's membership grew by 100,000 and the National Audubon Society, which seeks to protect birds, had a 44 percent
increase in membership. Friends of the Earth, the National
Resources Defense Council, and the Environmental Defense
Fund all showed sharp gains.

Clearly, the tide of public interest in the environment
was strong. Attempts to stonewall the situation—or even to
press for loosening environmental protection—not only were
unlikely to succeed; they "radicalized" more people to join
the environmental movement as activists. Yet trying to
weaken those protections was precisely what some heads of
corporations attempted. For example, efforts by some oil
companies to permit increased lead content in gasoline met
such opposition that the restrictions on lead were tightened,
even by a pro-business administration.

In the same way, it was the stonewalling tactics of the
Johnson and Nixon administrations on Vietnam that rallied
new millions to oppose that war.

Few situations threaten the very existence of an organization and require a fixed position. Therefore, an *objective*
reading of the climate can determine what the consequences

will be of various courses: adamance, modification, coalition, conciliation, or capitulation.

So a key question that must be asked when confronted with an opposing group whose case has merit—or that has such strong public support that it is unassailable at this time—is: How far should we go to accommodate?

Then these questions should follow:

- What are *your* options?

They may not only be standing firm, making various degrees of mutual adjustment, or capitulating. When Dow Chemical was faced with demands that it reduce effluents from its plants it developed ways not only to cut them but to turn some of the salvaged substances into salable products. Returns more than covered the costs of new equipment and technology.

- What are *their* options?

One of the tactics developed by activist groups is similar to mousetrapping in football. A position is taken that it has no expectation of attaining, but that it hopes will provoke the organization into making a mistake. Its objective is not to achieve that goal but to lead the organization into undermining its own support.

Lawsuits charging discrimination in hiring, for instance, were filed originally with little expectation of winning damages. Instead, they sought to provoke outbursts against "impractical radicals" and in defense of "management's right to choose personnel on the basis of qualifications." Regardless of the truth of those responses, they served to inflame many members of the large groups whose own high regard for their qualifications was being demeaned. Government officials and judges, conscious of the numbers in those groups, swung their support to the claimants.

What can the opponents do in response to each of the tactics that the organization may adopt? This kind of strategy checklist is much like a study of war games, except that victory is measured not in the number of square miles conquered but in the number of minds influenced.

• Who has viewpoints *different* from those of the activists?

These fall into two main categories: those who share the organization's views closely, and those who don't but who differ with the activists for other reasons. Both can become your allies.

One of the greatest weaknesses of the American competitive system is that it breeds a sense of competition in areas where it shouldn't exist. Only recently have unions and companies seen their mutual stake in forestalling extreme measures that shut down some industrial plants and so destroy jobs. The union and the company may disagree bitterly on whether reducing benefits would protect jobs against foreign competition; but they can agree that a law requiring 100 percent purity of water discharges would harm them both.

• Who offers *accepted avenues* for free discussion?

An organization under attack is usually the least credible source of counter material. It is talking in its own self-interest. It is a large institution, and therefore in our underdog-oriented society it is not admired. However deftly it moves, it is likely to be seen as throwing its weight around.

## Balancing the Weight of Information

It is vital to recognize that *it is not necessary to override the charges or claims of the dissidents.*

The first need is to prevent an imbalance in which the preponderant impressions on the issue are coming from the opponents. People generally do not favor action on a non-alarming situation when arguments seem to be balanced on both sides and there is a clear doubt.

Saul Alinsky—who inspired much of today's activist strategy—said: "Men will act when they are convinced their cause is 100 percent on the side of the angels and that the opposition are 100 percent on the side of the devil." On that basis, he justified using distortion, exaggeration, and lies to build a case—to prevent doubt.

The weight of impressions on the public must be balanced so people will have doubts and lack motivation to take action.

Accordingly, means are needed to get balancing information into the stream from sources that the public will find credible.

Those can be university-sponsored forums, church platforms or publications, respected publications or broadcast shows, or respected personages with no personal stake in the issue. All of these are likely to insist that the content contain the viewpoints of both sides. But since the vital need is to overcome a one-sided vacuum and to create a mixed picture so doubts will persist, that is a plus. The very care with which objectivity is maintained by these third parties helps foster credibility.

There is no need for a clear-cut "victory." In fact, a victory can backfire by providing the opponents with a rallying point, as we shall see in Chapter 13. The organization is being attacked in an effort to force undesired change. Nurturing public doubts by demonstrating that this is not a clear-cut situation in support of the opponents is all that is necessary. It will probably forestall the change.

- Can they be diverted elsewhere?

Activists are of two types: those who have a real personal grievance about the issue involved, and those who sought a grievance and settled on this one.

The first group includes blacks on issues affecting minority matters, or residents of a town where a nuclear power plant is proposed. They are not likely to be diverted, except by an even greater issue of personal concern. Many protesters against industrial development went mute when unemployment zoomed in 1982.

But the second group, as we shall see in Chapter 15, chooses an issue the way they choose a movie, on the basis of mood and convenience.

In 1972 Robert Choate, a civil engineer, gained instant fame by making unsupportable charges about breakfast cereals. Suddenly a movement sprung up, demanding that the government force cereal manufacturers to produce foods according to Choate's uninformed standards.

The strategy of the cereal industry was to stop being a lamb—an easy target—and become a porcupine—one that the attackers would soon learn offered few attractions. The industry's tactics gradually demonstrated that it was not an easy mark that would bring easy victory to the crusade-minded.

The opponents found that there were other, more attractive targets. They abandoned Choate and moved on to other causes. Except for reduced sugar content in a few cereals, none of the products was changed and the favorite breakfast food of millions of people has continued to be available.

## Advantage of the Moderate Approach

There is a centripetal force in American affairs. It resists polarization around any one point of view, but pulls all extremes in toward the center.

Extremist political parties have never gotten more than token votes in national elections.

Movements that have depended primarily on extremism have failed: leftist revolution (the IWW, the Symbionese Liberation Army, the Weathermen); Father Coughlin's call for a rightist uprising and Senator Joseph McCarthy's call for a red-baiting crusade; black revolution (the Black Panthers and others); takeovers of college deans' offices and bombing of college research buildings; bomb and terrorist attacks by forces seeking Puerto Rican independence or redressing the Armenian slaughter by Turks more than 70 years ago.

Extremist efforts to suppress mass movements have also failed: attacks on unionization in the 1930s, for example.

The key is that any extremist position is vulnerable. Americans are a temperate people; they are repelled by any excess. In a free society, all excesses create their own demise.

If the opposition is extremist, that is likely to be to your advantage rather than a serious long-term threat. The small group of women who became the visual symbols of the fight for the Equal Rights Amendment in 1982—some of whom chained themselves in the Illinois legislature and spilled blood on the historic inlaid marble floor—probably did more to prevent passage of the ERA than Phyllis Schlafly. The black students who brandished rifles while they took over the dean's office at Southern University were typical of the extremists who killed public support for "black studies" departments.

Basically, there are two kinds of pressure aimed at changing organizations and institutions—persuasion and force. The difference in their results is significant.

Persuasive efforts seek to capture the attention and acquiescence of an audience that can do something about the issue. They depend on organizing a strong case, catching attention for it, pushing it so it cannot be ignored, and being ready with practical proposals when receptivity has been attained. Marches and other visible tactics are persuasion, not force.

Force depends on frightening people, including the leaders who can take action. It relies on creating fear and on implied blackmail through threats of continued force if the demands are not met.

Since the American Revolution, few groups have gained their goals through the use of force. Recent movements that have succeeded through the use of persuasion include women's rights (except for the symbolic ERA), improved environment, noise abatement, greater attention to product safety, redesign of college enrollment and curricula, abortion liberalization, changes in elementary education, patients' rights, voting rights for blacks, and ending the Vietnam War.

As we've seen, movements based on force have failed. So when opponents' tactics use threats of force or actual force, the way is open to convert the organization's position from perceived tyrant to underdog.

However, it is vital that the organization avoid having itself cast into the position of using force or seeming to. For a large organization, seeming to use clout can be perceived as using force, because the power to get others to act on your behalf is interpreted by the general public as a power play.

A clash between dissidents, such as pickets outside a factory, and company guards may be initiated by the opponents, but the odds are overwhelming that it will be perceived as the powerful organization using its muscle on defenseless protesters.

Similarly, reports of heavy efforts by the organization to pressure legislators will be perceived as force. And so, often, are expensive ads opposing the dissidents' case, because they may be interpreted as efforts to outshout the unamplified voices of individuals who can't afford such ads.

In addition to avoiding being seen as using force, it is good strategy to reverse the pattern and put the onus of force on the opponents. Violence against employers' property during labor disputes leaches away public support for the strikers. Unions have learned that peaceful picketing makes them good guys, while clashes aimed at preventing other employees from getting to the job—or to keep the buses from running or the milk from being delivered—make their positions more difficult.

Others have not yet learned that lesson. The perception of anti-abortion advocates as dedicated people interested in God's laws and the sanctity of the individual received a blow when a fringe group apparently kidnapped an abortion doctor and his wife, after trying to burn down his house.

So the rules for dealing with opponents' legitimate

interests change when there are signs that the opponents are not legitimate—or will appear illegitimate in the eyes of the public.

An effective strategy is to disarm the critics by proving that the ogre they seek to depict doesn't exist. Following Alinsky's dictates, activists need not only seem to be 100 percent pure themselves but to have the targeted organization seem to be 100 percent evil.

Aggressive environmentalists depicted big chemical companies as insensitive polluters. When the Canadian Department of Agriculture planned to spray thousands of acres of timberland in the Eastern Provinces to destroy the spruce budworm, Dow Chemical Canada learned that its solvent would be used as the base—at a concentration of 75 percent. Dow had never made any tests on the safety of that solvent in such high proportions when used as a spray. The company immediately urged that the spraying not be done. Only when Dow chemists saw that tests made by the maker of the active insecticide, which was dissolved in the solvent, proved the mixture completely safe did it withdraw its objection. Government officials and newspapers hailed the judgment and responsibility of the company.

The company's action was immediate and effective because, after years of being attacked on various grounds, it had analyzed the patterns and developed a complete corporate policy not only on the use of its products by its own employees *and* by end-use processors, but on how to anticipate and handle situations that could have harmful repercussions.

More and more, looking ahead is becoming an essential point in overcoming opposition.

There are several steps in the process:

- Detect what "causes" or issues may be spawning opposition groups.
- Monitor their development by observing what is said in *their* media and in *their* meetings. By the time their views make the general public media they have already ma-

tured into movements and are much more difficult to deal with.

- Assess the issue's probable longevity. Is it a pesky quirk, such as demands for black studies (which hundreds of college administrators took seriously enough to disrupt their curricula and drain their budgets) or a real movement, such as the demand for equal job opportunities for women?

- Assess the nature and mood of the opposition group. Is this issue just a way station in its drive for continuous gratification or is it a purpose whose fulfillment will lead to the group's dissolution? If the members are basically the alienated, nothing will satisfy them. Meeting this challenge will only lead them to form new demands.

- Assess the long-term consequences. If agreement is reached and will not be followed by new demands, will the price be bearable *long into the future* as well as at the time of agreement?

    Companies faced with threatened boycotts by activist minority groups face that kind of decision: Will they severely weaken their ability to function competitively in years ahead by promoting unqualified people, appointing inept distributors, and employing agencies less able than those they would otherwise choose?

## The Procedure for Results

The process of dealing with legitimate forces, after these assessments and judgments, involves:

- Forming coalitions with legitimate groups whose interests are compatible on the issue. M.D.'s and osteopaths dispute each other constantly on matters of medical practice, but they have learned to support each other against activists who want to make all health practitioners dependent on the government. Arguments between professors of the humanities and career-preparation schools in universities are bitter. But when activists pressured to lower standards to make way for a quota of under-educated applicants for faculty positions, they closed ranks.

Many coalitions are less obvious. Often they are the kind of tradeoffs familiar in politics: One group supports another on one issue on which it has only a limited stake in return for support on another issue of importance to the first group. Farm groups have often worked with transportation companies to block inroads into the interests of both.

- Assuming the initiative on information about the issue. When a "cause" is surfacing, that is often the most critical time in determining its fate. Usually it emerges half-formed (if not half-baked) on the basis of a gripe or hunch of its originator. Like gaseous molecules about to form a star, the ideas whirl about seeking a core. That is the time when it is vital to get the most-authoritative and solid information into the consideration.

  In most cases the organization that would become the target of the "cause" has on its staff or available to it the best sources of information. By putting that information forward in the most effective forms, and seeing that it gets the widest dissemination and the most careful attention, the organization can forestall having to cope with legislation, a proposed regulation, or other inroads that would be based on specious inputs.

- Steering the focus of attention on the subject. This involves all the strategies and techniques of effective communication that will be treated in the last 16 chapters of this book.

- Giving the responsible members of the outside factions a sense of participation and letting them share in the progress made. Two groups can proceed up a staircase, though both at less speed and having to make accommodations; but to try to traverse a staircase in opposite directions can be exhausting and dangerous.

  People who have a purpose behind their actions, not just an unappeasable need to revolt, find the psychic lift they need in feeling themselves a part of a successful effort. Giving them a role in getting there not only makes it easier to make the adjustments agreed on; it can make allies out of those who would otherwise become enemies.

## CHAPTER 7

# Don't Let the Opponents Set the Agenda

THE MEDIA REVOLUTION SINCE 1955 has made who has the initiative in any encounter especially important.

The first burst of attention to a subject establishes how the public is likely to perceive it. That creates a mental imprint, like a photographic print on the memory, that becomes the basis on which all subsequent references to that subject are likely to be perceived.

For example, how blacks are treated in the South is still perceived by millions of people in light of television footage of the early 1960s showing crowds being held at bay by snarling dogs on leashes. Many things were not included in that imprint at the time; many things have changed since then. But the initiative created by black activists in provoking Southern policemen into using dogs is still the primary ingredient of public perception. The blacks set out to demonstrate how some Southern sheriffs treated them. The sheriffs

70

acted in character. The result was a history-changing impression on public attitudes.

Lessons are learned slowly—or not at all. The police in Chicago at the 1968 Democratic convention were instructed to take a passive position against the provocations of Yippies and other activists, whose strategy was to make themselves seem martyrs by provoking the police. Had the police continued to be passive—despite extreme provocations—the activists would have continued to be a mere sideshow of the convention. But the police let the activists create the perception of events—they were allowed to set the agenda for the public's consideration of the situation. The Yippies rioted first, but the result was that the scrape was labeled for all time "a police riot."

Activists have learned how to preempt the agenda for their causes by capturing the stage first and dictating the script. Often they literally put on an act to determine the course the scenario will take. As a result, time after time public issues have been forced into public consciousness and then pushed through the entire agenda of "consideration" to a conclusion without all the facts or the true consequences being considered.

Assuming the initiative in setting the agenda not only affords the massive advantage of imprinting the "cause" first and firmly. It also puts whoever is being criticized into a defensive position. The defense has to undo the first impression and seems always to be saying, "But that's not true; listen to us!"

In an age of electronic immediacy and visual impact, having always to *react* to others' initiatives is to seem *reactionary*.

All the avenues to people's minds—their own sense of curiosity, the media, the interest of those around them—are attuned to what is new or startling. That makes whatever is not new or what is merely a follow-up seem dull and weak.

A defensive position is therefore a position of weakness—in tactics and in the eyes of the people.

The audacious initiative of recent activists is exactly what plays best with the forces that shape public attitudes and therefore events—the media, emotion-oriented people who are seeking outlets for their frustrations or urges to change the world, and the power leaders in legislative, administrative, and judicial circles.

During the period in which the shift in power has occurred, the media have been revolutionized. Now media devoted to thoughtfulness and careful consideration have minuscule circulation and most of them are short-lived. Media with vast audiences and great impact on attitudes are creatures of immediate sensation and superficiality.

A thoughtful biography of George Washington fills several large volumes; television condenses the whole American Revolution into a one-hour (really 52-minute) special.

Worldwide efforts to superheat economies to meet everyone's desires have hundreds of roots and damage hundreds of millions of people; television shows three or four poor people whose welfare payments are cut and concludes that budget-trimming is inhumane.

It is this susceptibility to sensation and superficiality that makes it so important how each issue gets onto the public agenda. The media, and people who have grown up to encapsulate their thinking as the media do, make it easy to gain attention for sensational charges with shallow foundations. It is extremely difficult—as well as far less effective—to balance the judgments.

In early times many media themselves had great influence on the evolution of public attitudes. A thoughtful article in *The Atlantic*, a thorough series in *The New York Times*, or a feature in *Reader's Digest* could form opinion and create results. One pioneer in public relations described how in the '20s he helped a New York hotel overcome a rumor campaign started by a dissident group. The rumors indicated the hotel was about to close. Reservations dropped. Long-time residents began to look for accommodations elsewhere. He advised the hotel to hire a famous chef, who obviously would demand a large salary. The story appeared in the New York newspapers. The rumor died. The dissident group was thwarted.

In 1982 the nation's biggest advertiser, Procter & Gamble, was confronted by rumors so unfounded that thoughtful people laughed at them—that P & G was a supporter of the devil. Yet all its resources and efforts—including massive media coverage—had great difficulty in blunting the virulence of the rumors.

The media today are not so much the architects of public attitudes as gatekeepers of the agenda for what the public considers.

Once an issue has "made" the media it is likely to have momentum. If it has the potential for dispute and agitation it is likely to stay on the agenda until it loses the ability to agitate, it results in action that changes the situation, or it is transformed by the interplay of debate. And once it's on the agenda, any organization at which the issue is aimed is likely to be on the defensive.

## Agenda-Setting Tactics

Clearly, it is in an organization's interest to have the initiative in setting the agenda on issues that concern it, or at least to blunt efforts of opponents to preempt the agenda. To have a chance to do that, it's important to look at the sources of opposition and how they grasp for the initiative in setting the agenda.

Sy Kahn, in *Organizing*, cites tactics used most often:

- Strikes
- Picket lines
- Public hearings
- Press conferences
- Visits to public officials
- Mass demonstrations
- Petitions
- Boycotts
- Sit-ins
- Confrontations
- Paid advertising
- Staged actions
- Marches
- Letters

- Exposés
- Silent vigils
- Rallies
- Prayer services
- Civil disobedience
- Legal actions

He does not include other types of attention-grabbing efforts that Saul Alinsky advocated: disrupting solemn meetings in legislatures or churches, hurling insults at speakers to provoke ejections, dumping sewage on immaculate property of the attacked organization, disrupting operations with fake bomb threats, and the like.

By observing emerging opposition groups—by getting as close to their members as feasible, by studying their publications, by talking to others who have encountered them—it is possible to predict what type of tactics they will use.

Organizers of dissidents have learned that it is not effective to call on people to do things that are outside their experience or sense of propriety: Thoughtful people concerned about the safety of their homes are not likely to join a campaign to prevent a school from functioning, let alone plant bombs.

"An early choice of tactics for a young organization," says Kahn, "might include petitions, writing letters and negotiating sessions which are not too confrontational. When these fail to produce results, the same group will often become much more open to creating pressure on the opposition through direct action tactics such as sit-ins, picket lines, mass demonstrations, marches, and strikes."

The early tactics are not the type that set agendas. If the organization is approached with one or more of them, it has an early signal—a chance to dispose of the issue or to take the initiative to block the group's next efforts that *would* set the public agenda.

It is important to note that most of Kahn's list of *activist* tactics depend little on facts or the merits of the case. Many, in fact, depend on abusing uninvolved outsiders into carrying out the group's purposes, as when activists systematically stall lines before tellers' windows at banks to make the banks' officers put pressure on their customer, the targeted organization. A similar tactic involves strikes that greatly inconvenience the public—failure to collect garbage, immobilizing buses or trains, closing schools—rather than allow the negotiations to be settled on their merits.

Often it is the situation that is least related to the merits, in fact, that most readily captures the public agenda. And it is such cases that sometimes refute the usual rule that the agenda-setter has the great advantage.

A group that overplays its role by outraging the public—such as the air controllers' union in 1981—gives the target a chance to assume the position of underdog or martyr, and so to prevail.

## Whom Do They Represent?

Implicit in the agenda-grabbing process is the assumption that the group taking the initiative represents "the public interest." Virtually every activist group in democratic countries starts with at least the implied assertion that it is the chosen instrument of a substantial body of people who have been abused or neglected by some arrogant power.

It declares that only by joining this group can the public gain its rights. Often the word *Public* is embodied in the group's name. Since everyone knows he or she is a member of the Public, even though they don't feel deprivation or abuse on the question involved, people tend to be unquestioning about which side to be on.

Actually, of more than 1,000 public interest groups identified by the Foundation for Public Affairs, only a handful—such as the Audubon Society and the Sierra Club—had enough members to win an election in just one of the 435 Congressional districts. The leaders of none of the public interest groups have been elected in a democratic process that represents all people affected. Then the groups unhesitatingly say they speak for vast numbers of people.

The Conservation Council of Ontario, for instance, claimed that through representatives of its 37 member organizations it spoke for well over a million Ontario citizens in proposing legislation. But one of the 37 groups was the Ontario Medical Association. No one had ever polled the doctors of the OMA on that legislation and most of them had probably never heard of the CCO.

Jeffery M. Berry, a political scientist at Tufts University, found that 30 percent of the groups who claimed to speak for the public had no members at all. T. R. Reid of *The Washington Post* estimated that half the groups had no members.

Numbers and bodies are two potent tools in the struggle for authority.

For many years politicians have employed or induced people to make up crowds at their rallies.

Activists have bribed police officials to grossly overestimate crowd counts at protest meetings—and established organizations have used their influence to play down the crowd estimates.

Some women's organizations claim they speak for an overwhelming majority of women, while the actual majority of the population composed of women votes resoundingly for male candidates against their feminine opponents. (The number of female office holders increases as the number of candidates who most voters—male and female—feel are qualified for the jobs increases.)

For years activists played on the hunger of the media for numbers and bodies—the substance of "visual reality" in human affairs. If they had only a small group at a demonstration, they made it suitable for TV by adding theater—aggressive statements, figures burned in effigy, dummies of babies alleged to have starved. TV cameras focused on these and never used full-angle views that would have shown the paucity of people involved in the supposed outbursts of public outrage.

Thus, playing the numbers game is a primary technique

for setting the agenda on an issue. It is ironic that the leaders of organizations—whose orientation is heavily toward numbers—have so often been impaled on these tricks with numbers.

One of the first steps in assessing an opposing group is to audit its numbers. How many people does it *really* represent—represent to the extent that those people will take action on the basis of this issue?

Although its claim that it speaks for most American women is exaggerated, National Organization for Women (NOW) *does* have a substantial constituency that can be counted on to vote for or against a candidate on the basis of a women's-interest issue. On the other hand, for years Ralph Nader claimed to represent American consumers when his only real potency was a genius for provoking media attention to his attacks. His numbers were small, but it was a mistake, made by General Motors and others, to assume that he therefore could not assert influence.

So a second step is to assess what the potency of the opponents is in terms of *what they can make happen*. Only a minute percentage of parishioners really cared about some churchmen's campaign against Nestlé Company because it sold infant formula in Africa. But because the churchmen aroused the evangelical passion of a few parishioners, pressure on Nestlé and its subsidiaries caused the company, after long resistance, to change the format of its sales practices.

## Interlocking Groups

That case revealed how opposition movements not only interact, but sometimes get supporters of activist causes involved in far more than they intend. Largely because of church-inspired activism against the sale of infant formula in countries with problems of sanitation and poverty, a chain of worldwide movements was uncovered. The infant formula controversy broke into world consciousness when the UNrelated World Health Organization pushed through a Code that would give non-medical bureaucrats in all countries the right to dictate how the medical profession must treat babies. The issue was presented with such emotion and unreason that many nations' representatives, rather than seem to be opposing protection of babies, shrugged and voted for the Code. Only the United States held to its principles and refused to commit itself to a Code it could not follow.

Examination of that emotion-laden event led to further revelations.

Countries of the world that, after millenia, had never achieved economic stability were pushing to force on all advanced countries a New International Economic Order—in which bureaucrats with no proved success in running an economy would dictate economic decisions for all countries.

A new Law of the Sea was about to be signed, giving countries that had never developed their own waterways or the mineral wealth beneath their feet the right to full shares in all wealth taken from the seas.

It was efforts to push through a New International Communication Order that brought all of these related maneuvers to public attention. When the media awoke to what this Information Order would do to strangle freedom of news reporting, the machinations ceased being separate, arcane diddling around the (yawn) UN tables and were seen as grabs for world control of health care, the economy, the world's resources, and the free flow of information.

This is an example not only of how small activist-minded groups can claim to speak for the people (no working mothers in Kenya were consulted before the ban on ready availability of infant formulas was proposed). It also shows how vital it is to explore movements for their offshoots and tie-ins.

Some of these have become visible, such as the readiness of homosexual groups, prostitutes, and farm laborers to join each other's demonstrations. Others are not visible until they are carefully tracked, such as the alliance between unions representing millions of consumers and employers in the auto and textile industries to raise prices to Americans by imposing trade restrictions on imports.

Some reveal surprising contradictions, such as the early joining of pro-abortion and anti-abortion groups of women in agitation against infant formulas. Pro-abortionists fight for the woman's right to make her own choices—but found themselves advocating that bureaucrats have the right to tell them how they should feed their children. Anti-abortionists fought for the preservation of every child from conception on—but found themselves approving controls that would result in the death of many babies who could not be adequately nourished by their mothers.

The agenda is often set by the use of emotion and avoiding full consideration of the consequences of proposals. The attack on "redlining"—the practice of lending institutions to restrict loans in areas where they would be least likely to receive repayment—got onto the agenda as outrage against limiting low-income people who wanted to buy homes. Just as people who had a lot of accidents had to be allowed to buy insurance rather than be denied the right to drive (resulting in involuntary raises in insurance costs to safe drivers and a boost in the highway death rate) so people who were least likely to repay had to be given mortgage loans—resulting in higher losses, which weakened the financial strength of lenders, which led to higher mortgage rates, which contributed to millions of responsible Americans finding it almost impossible to buy homes.

The emotional appeal of such causes carries great impact. When the agenda began with outrage about people not being allowed to buy homes because of where they live, the logic of the consequences of prohibiting redlining did not prevail.

A more recent example is the outcry against "gentrification"—movement of responsible people into run-down neighborhoods to rehabilitate old buildings and create viable neighborhoods. The agenda has been almost set by the emotional outcry that poor people are being forced to move away. The fact that nothing can be made better except by those who can improve it may be unable to get a hearing in the clamor of people who over decades presided over the creation of the slum.

## Hearings As "Show Trials"

Every element of democracy that is intended to benefit the powerless has been perverted, at times, into a means of grasping power. Nowhere is that more evident than in public hearings.

A public hearing often sets the public agenda on the issue it is designed to air.

The purpose of hearings is to open the deliberations of government bodies to public review. Many do, from considering whether a village should close a dog pound to a Senate discussion of nuclear arms. But there are two forms of abuse of their purpose that counteract open consideration of issues:

1. By their nature, public hearings cater to the atmosphere of anti-leadership. Their purpose is to forestall any tendency of elected or appointed officials to misappropriate their power, to the public's disadvantage. (Secondarily, they are supposed to provide those officials with broadened knowledge of the facts; but a hearing is a far less efficient means than thoughtful study of documented information received in other forms.)

Accordingly, there tends to be an atmosphere of distrust that hangs over many hearings before the first gavel. In these cases the officials are on the defensive from the start.

2. The public hearing is a created event, and so gets onto the docket of the media. That makes it a ready device for trying to seduce the media.

Interest groups see it as a fine pulpit for propounding

their views, with little need to be disciplined by either facts or decorum. Media coverage is overwhelmingly a reflex: reporting what is said and done, not checking on its validity or implications.

On the other hand, those who call the hearing are also likely to use it as a springboard to media attention. Their inherent ego and political ambitions find in the hearing an alluring opportunity.

In fact, the only purpose of many hearings is to create media events. Senator Joseph McCarthy used them early in his rampage to national prominence—and was brought down by his excesses at his committee's hearings on alleged Communists in the army. Senator Estes Kefauver orchestrated hearings on organized crime and the pharmaceutical industry—playing up a new "revelation" just in time for each day's news deadlines, scheduling witnesses so the most sensational ones (previously coached) got the play and the responsible ones were lost in the routine.

Such hearings provide much the same purpose as Russian "show trials," where the result is foreordained and all the testimony is entirely for propaganda.

This technique for capturing the public agenda can be devastating to the target organization. Thwarting it calls for sophisticated planning and action:

1. Each hearing should be sized up thoroughly as soon as it is scheduled:

- What are the motives of all those involved—the officials who called the hearing; other agencies or bodies involved; witnesses who are scheduled; other groups with a stake in the subject who may try to obstruct, distort, shout down or otherwise affect the proceedings?

- What traps must be watched out for? What trick questions might be asked? What phony accusations? How might the questioner imply wrongdoing and cut off any chance to offer corrective information? What might be done to provoke your anger—just when the TV cameras and reporters are alerted?

- What might you do to neutralize would-be opponents at the hearing? What evidence can be ready to demonstrate the weakness of their arguments or the irresponsibility of their actions?

- Size up the media situation and make thorough plans to deal with it:

    ¶Make advance contact with the specific media that will probably be interested in the hearings and with their subject matter.

    ¶See what each medium's attitude is. Alert its staff to the upcoming hearings, their significance, and the nuances involved.

    ¶Try to affect their attitude and to alert them to what the opponents are likely to try, so they can be on guard.

    ¶Encourage or discourage coverage of the hearings by providing information about their importance or validity.

    ¶Provide information and/or an interview subject (and an interviewee) that can set the tone for the medium's approach, save the reporters' time in covering the hearings, and help assure a fair treatment for your position.

    ¶Be sure to provide thorough and careful service to the media during the hearings.

## Preparing to Control the Agenda

All of these testify to the importance of detecting when an issue is likely to be put forward and of being prepared with the facts and sound arguments *before* the charges splash onto the agenda.

The basic process required includes these steps:

1. Have an information-detecting function always operating to detect *in advance* what some activist group may bring forth. That calls for being in touch with people *inside*

the publics that give birth to such movements. Check their media—the alternate press, scholarly journals in the social sciences, anti-establishment publications. Watch the mail for hints of new complaints. Be objective and leave traditional thinking in abeyance. A few years ago hardly anyone would have taken seriously an effort to force compensation scales based on "equal value of work," relating such dissimilar jobs as a plumber and a teacher of history.

2. Have the facts scrupulously researched and documented in advance—on every subject that the monitoring process flushes out.

3. Identify the group that is germinating the issue. Identify its actual backers. Identify its actual or likely allies. Know what their track record has been, their strengths, their vulnerabilities among reasonable people.

4. Inoculate the channels of influence against readily accepting what the activists will charge. Those channels include the media, government, academia, and those who will have a stake in the issue, such as employees whose jobs may be jeopardized, customers whose costs may be raised, or mothers whose children may be denied security or opportunity.

Alert them to the emergence of the issue.

Watch for the "movement" to come into the open.

Immediately provide facts, perspective, and implications. Especially spell out the consequences of allowing the activists' position to prevail.

5. Become the dependable source of information at the *formation* stage of awareness. That should help inoculate the influence centers against accepting distorted, half-baked, or simplistic assertions and provide a basis for reasoned consideration of the issue.

6. Set up scenarios on what the opponents are likely to do. Try to be prepared for all of them.

7. Determine who else has a viewpoint opposed to the activists. Who else might be hurt by irresponsible moves re-

sulting from their cause? Who might be your allies on this issue because of their own concerns or to have you as an ally on some other issue?

8. Get those who have reason to oppose the activists to join in helping set the agenda. Hold conferences. Educate the media. Educate educators. Inform government officials and personnel.

9. Keep your eye on the key goal: Prevent your foes from setting and keeping the agenda. Make the agenda cover the *full* scope of the subject: People are not likely to take sides when there is no clear-cut side to take. Where there is a range of arguments on a subject, and none stands out, people have the instinct that there is no clear cause that needs their attention.

# CHAPTER 8

# Make the Media Play It Straight

THE MEDIA HAVE BECOME MORE IMPORTANT as gatekeepers of the public agenda than as actual creators of change. But that does not lessen their importance to every organization and institution that seeks to function in an orderly manner.

The media are predisposed toward activism and support for forces antagonistic to the stability of established institutions because of the nature of journalism, the nature of the media business, and the nature of editorial people.

It is axiomatic that things that are established are not news. What is familiar seldom stirs curiosity in an audience, so it holds little interest for those who write or broadcast. It is not oversimplifying to say that the nature of journalism inevitably creates a bias against stability.

Accordingly, there is built in an eagerness for changes being made, about to be proposed, or alleged to be needed.

Science news, for instance, does not deal with miracles already wrought and in place. It plays up new theories or techniques that may topple established theories or techniques.

The business of the media is a paradox: On one hand it is a business—usually exceptionally lucrative—that wants as much as any business to function without hindrance or incursions. On the other hand, it is dependent for its revenue on grasping the attention and continued interest of the largest audience it can. Both its circulation and its advertising revenues make it vital that it capture the audience. To do so it must do what interests audiences, which is to probe and attack what is established.

Few media, aside from specialized journals, hesitate to put the audience-luring functions ahead of the feelings of the advertisers, whenever a disparity might exist. And if the medium really fulfills its function for the advertiser, few advertisers can refuse to give it their dollars.

The nature of editorial people, as we shall see, further loads the public agenda on the side of activists. People who choose careers in the creative aspects of journalism tend to reject the hard-headed and highly competitive careers in other fields—business, administration of health centers or colleges, the armed forces, and so on. They are moved not by tangible measurements but by enticing ideas. They feel that because of their ability to grasp broad concepts and ideas they are the highest level of society; yet much greater rewards go to their opposites, the leaders of organizations and institutions. They have a "divine discontent" that is a necessary trait of all truly creative people.

The period during which the focus of power has shifted coincides with a major revolution among the media.

The massive rise of television and related electronic techniques, plus an explosion of special-interest publications and other new media, has had a massive impact on the role of the media themselves. In some ways they have become more potent in their influence on events. As the public has become much more segmented, the mass media have an enhanced effect: They form a net that somewhat covers the diverging interests of people being splintered into thousands of work specialties, hundreds of causes, innumerable lifestyles, scattered locations.

At the same time, much of their potency has been diluted by segmentation among the media. Only the *Reader's Digest* remains of the once-powerful magazines of general interest. Now there is a multitude of special-interest publications, from *Gun Digest* and *Beekeepers Journal* to *Working Mother*. The fastest growing magazines of general circulation focus on one city or area. The number of daily metropolitan newspapers dwindles while suburban and area papers thrive.

The grip of the three television networks is slipping as cable TV, pay TV, videotapes, and syndicated programming grow. Radio is prosperous but splintered into many types of voices, most of them focusing on music rather than on information and ideas.

This paradox of both increased impact and scattered influence is the reality faced by leaders of organizations when considering how the media will influence events.

## Understanding the Media Today

Many factors have been responsible for dramatic changes in the communications media during the past generation. A common mistake of organization leaders is to consider the media as if they were still like those when the leaders were growing up.

● Many conditions are pressuring the media to compete for attention. The audience is less able to read. It is less willing to read. Even the electronic media, which supposedly bypass reading, suffer because people's ability to think and associate ideas is related to their ability to read and to focus their thoughts.

There has been a multiplication of media, with TV, audio cassettes, TV tapes, video games, special-interest publications, and other new media more than replacing the disappearance of some mass magazines and newspapers. In addition, the activities available to people have grown substantially, competing for their time and attention.

The result is that simplistic, shallow, attention-grabbing impacts are needed to lure people to any medium, and their attention is likely to be lost if this superficiality is alleviated to provide meaty material.

That has made many media susceptible to sensationalism.

David Dellinger, one of the leaders of activist groups of the 1960s, explained why they developed irresponsible tactics to grasp public attention:

"The jaded, voyeuristic public gets interested—for a moment—when there is a corpse, a secret lover, a payoff. It's hard to drum up interest in anything . . . fundamental."

Media people tend to rail at this kind of criticism—but they made panderers of sensation over substance, such as Dellinger, Abby Hoffman, Huey Newton, William Kunstler, Stokely Carmichael, and Jesse Jackson, among the best-known personages in America.

● The nature of media people has changed. It used to be that the proprietor of a medium expressed his viewpoint. With the ascendance of professionally trained journalists and their unions, editorial staffers have major control over content. And both their origins and their interpretation of the role of journalism have been revolutionized.

In 1982, when two-thirds of Americans said they were conservative, a poll of media people showed that 54 percent identified themselves as liberals and only 8 percent as conservative. In 1976 when voters were almost exactly divided between President Ford and Jimmy Carter, media people favored Carter by a margin of 81 percent to 19 percent.

Where previously people entered journalism because they thought it offered a career for creative people, after

Woodward and Bernstein were converted by their Watergate exposé into personages and millionaires, journalism schools were swamped with young people who saw journalism as a means to remake the world in their image and get rich besides. A national poll of media people found them unblushingly saying that the group that should have the power to run society was media people.

• The unquestioned autonomy of the media—once the only group in America answerable to no one—has been transformed. Refusal of media people to cooperate in providing testimony against killers led courts to hold reporters accountable. Extreme instances of television programs concocting "news" and falsifying footage to make a story come out the way they wanted led to sharp drops in public confidence. More than a third of people said they found coverage faulty on stories with which they were familiar. The widely held attitude of media people that the First Amendment justified any actions they chose was widely considered self-serving arrogance.

Not only courts have breached the impregnable cloak around the media. A National News Council was formed to publicly review complaints about distortion. The Media Institute now offers objective critiques. Accuracy in Media acts as a strident gadfly. There are both national and local reviews in journalism. Though the most arrogant newspapers and networks have been the loudest in objecting to anyone having any say over journalistic practices, the pattern is set: Even a number of media themselves have employed ombudsmen with some authority to investigate complaints. Previously intransigent networks have begun to make retractions or offer apologies for the grossest distortions.

• Media and their influence are being decentralized.

What technology caused in the past century technology is now undoing. The telegraph, railroads, telephone, automobile, airlines, and television all worked to transform a vast land of many regions and towns into a unified whole.

The entire nation became the market for mass-produced goods—and the audience for mass-produced communication. Communications could be disseminated quickly to everyone, so they could originate wherever technology was available. That led to centering communication sources in a small area of Manhattan, with specialized segments in Washington, Los Angeles, and Chicago.

The new wave of technological advance is reversing the trend. The fastest growing segments of the magazine business are regional and special-interest publications. The greatest areas of expansion in TV are cable, satellite transmission, and videotapes, all of which are geared to local interest much more than network TV is. The decline in readership of newspapers is being met by greater attention to local needs and interests.

• They are also being diversified, weakening the individual medium's impact. The explosion in the number of media—even in the face of fewer newspapers in each city—has thinned out the audience reached by any one.

## Getting Them to Play It Straight

With this understanding of the importance of the media and how they are positioned today, there are a number of things an organization can do to optimize the treatment it receives:

1. Assess the media that will be involved with your organization and issues likely to face it. This assessment must be done medium by medium, rather than as a group. Although there is much lockstep coverage by various media, it is not safe to generalize.

In each case assess how the medium has treated the organization in the past; its essential fairness or susceptibility to being suckered by extremists when approaching new subjects; the background and maturity of its editorial staff people; its concern for its reputation for accuracy and fairness; and what its own stake is in the welfare of the organization.

What is your organization's status and credibility with each medium? What are the medium's prejudices? What is its relationship with leaders of activist groups you may be confronting?

2. When a new issue seems to be emerging, assess each medium in terms of how it is likely to treat it. Do its staff people have a stake in what activist groups will bring up? What is its record in handling similar matters recently?

3. Establish accessibility *in advance* to the key gatekeepers of news coverage at each medium. Get acquainted with the pertinent editors—business, environment, city, or others. Establish an understanding about the organization's functions, its concerns about the community and the public, its concern that coverage of any issue be objective, its readiness to answer questions and provide information, and so on. Establish your reliability as a source by answering all inquiries fully and promptly even on matters of little importance or unrelated to the organization's interests.

4. Humanize your organization. Let the media get to know and respect *people*, rather than trying to have them deal with an institution. Leaders of the organization should become known, seen, heard, and respected.

5. Seed the flow of information on the emerging issue in advance. Develop authoritative, sound, fair material on the subject that is better than anyone else can produce. Make it available in personal contacts and by delivery to key people at every medium on the list you have developed. Encourage inquiries, requests for materials, discussions. Be sure that no objective person or organization can draw up a proposal on what concerns you without incorporating what you have to offer.

6. Become the key reliable source on the subject. Be sure that whenever any medium covers the subject it's likely

to think of you first, or at least hesitate to complete its coverage without contacting you.

7. Establish visibility. Do things about the subject in question that command respectful attention. Preempt the front of the stage on that subject.

8. Hold media people responsible. When media were unassailable it often was fruitless to protest shabby treatment. That has changed. The multiple forms of scrutiny now being focused on media people make them sensitive to what can damage their esteem.

Aside from money, probably the most precious asset of the journalist is the esteem of his or her peers. That esteem is augmented when major stories are achieved but diminished when the methods used are shown to be shabby. This concern for the respect of peers is the most available channel for preventing shabby treatment.

Use fair and objective means to show your organization will fight such treatment. Protest first to the journalist and request redress. If that fails, protest to his or her boss. If that's unsuccessful, then consider "going public."

If that decision is made, develop a scrupulously accurate, thoroughly documented demonstration that the treatment was irresponsible—not just routinely inaccurate. The offense must be glaring to gain a sympathetic hearing for a rebuttal. Don't aim to embarrass anyone. Just set the record straight and make it clear that you will respond to any other such off-base attacks. Become known among media people as a porcupine rather than a rabbit.

Traits of this type have been proved at least partially effective by organizations as Kaiser Aluminum when it was refused time to rebut network accusations about its aluminum being unsafe in electric wiring; by Illinois Power Company, which distributed uncut footage of interviews by "60 Minutes" to demonstrate distortion; by Mobil Oil, W. R. Grace, Ralston Purina, and others.

The mass media are like cameras that are supposed to

give people a picture of the world. What passes through their shutters forms a picture that is imprinted on many minds. What a camera reproduces may be only a small part of the real world, or a distorted picture of it. So it is with the media. It is vital that every organization learn how to optimize the chances that the pictures provided to the public will be clear, representative, and fair.

# SECTION THREE

# Strategy

# CHAPTER 9

# Organizing for Effectiveness

MANY LEADERS OF ORGANIZATIONS who plan meticulously each item of the budget and each minute of the annual meeting leave to chance what happens in the arena of external events.

The last portion of the twentieth century is dominated by the human climate, which determines every organization's ability to function and even its right to exist. No decision made by any organization can be isolated from that human climate—and the efforts of activists are aimed at changing it. Neglecting to give major attention to such efforts is comparable to neglecting to provide a shelter when winter approaches.

To be in command of the changing climate instead of being buffeted by it requires, first of all, consciousness of this vital fact: Everything that the organization plans will depend on how it sizes up and deals with pressures coming from outside.

Required are:

1. Awareness by the organization's leaders that there no longer is a choice. It is not possible to ignore serious pockets of opposition.

The low profile is a luxury that has ceased to exist for virtually all organizations. The organization cannot hide behind cloistered walls or barricades of privacy. The new activist-media force is the "smart bomb" of our modern social system. It is able to seek out what were previously low-profile organizations and institutions and attack them. Thousands of groups and firms that "minded their own business" for years have found themselves blasted in their once-impregnable bunkers.

2. Recognition that mastering this aspect of the organization's affairs is as major as any other. It requires the best available orientation, knowledge, and skills just as much as finance, operations, or marketing.

3. Consideration of how outside groups will respond and what the organization may face from them must be fundamental in all decision-making. A university can no longer plan to build a physics laboratory and then decide how to announce it. A company can't decide to shift what it produces at a given plant before it considers what the community, the employees, the schools, consumer groups, the local business community, and others will feel.

4. Experience, judgment, skills, and resources must be structured into the organization. They are not facilities to be called on in case of need, like doctors and hospitals, but indispensable elements.

Next should be a careful weighing of the posture to be taken. Just as the nature of the populace has changed dramatically, so has the way organizations should think of it. Increasing sophistication has modified how organizations approach their relations with various groups.

There have been three major conceptions of that role:

1. *To master the publics*, to direct what they should think and do, according to the desires of the organization. This is the action approach that perceives the publics as targets of the organization's self-interest. It was the predominant way organizations were oriented when institutions had unquestioned dominance in society. It is occasionally the necessary course when an organization faces an adversary whose demands are untenable or destructive. In such cases firmness in support of the organization's principles or purposes is judicious.

2. *To block and parry*, to react to developments and problems, to respond to events or the initiatives of others by blunting them. This "low profile" approach was prominent during the era when all organizations were considered private entities, responsible only to their members or stockholders. There are occasions when a low profile is judicious to avoid having an issue or an adversary's maneuvers turned into sensation.

3. *To achieve mutual adaptation*, to develop relationships of mutual benefit to all parties. Where the activist group is sincere, even though intemperate, this is the desired approach. No. 1 or No. 2 should be considered where sober judgment indicates No. 3 cannot be effective.

## Setting Up the Structure

Organizing for this function includes:

● Appointing to the board of directors at least one member who has strong orientation toward public attitudes. Boards are traditionally composed of practical-minded people in the case of corporations, or public-spirited people in the case of health organizations and public service institutions. Needed is someone who combines the instincts of a master politician for public reaction with the disciplined thinking of an effective manager, to incorporate what is realistic and attainable within the organization's situation.

● Having a key executive on the staff who has a strong background in public relations and public affairs. That type of person—if blessed with a good mind and judgment—will consider all aspects dealt with in this book. He or she will also develop strategy, plans, and activities to carry out the functions needed.

● Establishing a process for monitoring what is developing among the publics that may have an impact on the organization. "You don't need a weatherman to know which way the wind is blowing," Woody Guthrie said. But you do need weathervanes. Every organization needs a continuing ear for what is being said and an eye for what is being written or shown where its interests are involved.

That includes participation in various groups, reading the special-interest and underground press, reviewing the intellectual journals where new ideas are given their tentative flights, and talking with ministers and others who have the ear of their followers.

Often the publications of activist groups will clearly describe its intended actions and timetable. *Liberation*, a magazine devoted to social activism, carried an article about plans to confront Honeywell Corporation months before the confrontation.

Often organizers of movements have to publicly stake out their targets in advance to stir up interest among the followers they seek.

● Establishing liaison with public-issue groups and the public. Except when the group is overtly hostile and considers holding discussions to be pandering to the enemy, liaison can provide not only early information about what's on in its mind. Often it can resolve any questions before they mature into issues.

It is in such liaison that the organization sometimes is

able to demonstrate that it would be a porcupine on the matter being considered.

- Getting the highest caliber of input from one or more experts outside the organization. People within are inevitably oriented to its psyche and history. Someone is needed who has the interest of the organization in mind but who can bring it objectivity and a wide range of diverse experience and skills.

- Setting up a process for watching the general media to see what subjects arise and show signs of becoming issues.

- Establishing liaison with all media that may be interested in topics of concern to the organization. This will open up mutual awareness and open the way for the media to call on the organization as a source at early stages of any development.

- Setting up guidelines and procedures to make leaders of the organization accessible and knowledgeable for the media.

Detailed guidelines for setting up the structure and carrying out activities are provided in Chapter 22.

# CHAPTER 10

# Approach: Self-Interest of the Audience

To THE LEADER OF ALMOST ANY ORGANIZATION, it is the predominant interest in his life, after his or her family. So it is natural that wherever the organization's interests are concerned he sees things from its viewpoint. The tendency of everyone to overbalance his attention toward what is in his interest is augmented by this dominance of the organization in his mind.

The fact is, though, that hardly anyone else cares about the organization. Yes, its employees want their jobs, its suppliers want it as a customer, and its members or stockholders recognize they have a stake in it. But even they see it as only a means to fulfill their interests. Leaders constantly despair over how hard it is to get employees, suppliers, and members or stockholders to pay attention to their messages.

The strength of the organization—the synergistic powers it attains through structure and size—is a disadvantage in gaining the support of people. An organization is a monolith, an institution. It is not seen as a human entity. So it does not strike a human rapport with those it deals with.

This is compounded by the penchant of managers to fulfill their own urge for solidity. They name their organizations with dehumanized labels, such as International Institutions Incorporated; and then "simplify" it into either Eyeco or III, draining any bit of human association out of it. The decline in the number of companies and other institutions bearing a person's name is indicative of the gradual dehumanization of the world of organizations. As medical centers take on institutional names, they lose the sense of humanity that a doctor's name has. Hospitals' names denote their reach—Massachusetts General—rather than the sense of people providing service, such as Mayo Clinic. The swing of college predominance from the Harvard, Yale, Stanford identity with founders to a welter of state institutions has paralleled the growing aura of impersonality that people object to. There may be no connection at all between the name and the actual sensitivity of the organization to people—but the institutional name does add to its employees' sense of impersonality.

Lacking rapport is a two-way handicap: The organization is too self-centered to recognize that issues will be determined by what people feel they will gain; and people are far more inclined to side with a group of people than with a monolithic organization in any dispute. They will hear with less critical judgment and more emotion what is said by people than what comes from an organization.

That is the crux of activists' advantage. They can readily establish a "we" relationship with most audiences, including the decision-takers in government. They can assume the posture of "people like us" and "we're in this together."

Thus, when International Harvester was on the brink of bankruptcy, the interest of people in Fort Wayne and Springfield, Ohio, was not in the fate of this company founded by the inventor of the reaper. It was what would happen to their jobs, their stores, their cities' tax revenues. Both workers and their neighbors listened to all the reasons coming from the unions about why wages should not be cut, even though it was obvious to others that the only hope of the workers was to cut them.

This follows the first precept of dealing with people: You must focus on what's in it for them.

Orientation of leaders must start with understanding the viewpoint of the audiences. The focal point of preventing opposition is to bite your tongue before you say "we" and train yourself to say "they." When talking with others, the question is "What do you want?" not "How can we get what we want?" We're most likely to get what we want if the publics feel their interests are being addressed.

The topic may still be: "How can this new waste disposal plant be approved?" But in approaching the question, attention will start with why the people in the community should approve it for *their* benefit. A woman can understand that she has to have some way of disposing of her garbage—and so must a hospital or a factory—whereas she's not likely to respond to arguments about the hospital or company having problems if the waste disposal plant is barred.

## Orienting to Others' Interests

Orientation to the viewpoints of others is needed in three directions:

1. With opponents and potential opponents. We have reviewed the nature of opposition and how opponents' groups operate. It is clear that plugging into the interests of the people they appeal to before they do is the best means of preventing opposition from jelling.

2. With the publics that will be appealed to:

• Government—legislative, regulatory, judicial.

Elected officials have highly sensitive antennae. They are tuned to whatever will have a bearing on their chances for reelection or advancement to higher positions. Showing how the position of the organization can further that ambition is far more important than talking about what will happen to the organization.

The politician cares much more about 500 voters who happen to work for a supermarket chain than about the same 500 people in their role as employees.

A bureaucrat cares about (1) avoiding waves that may mar his or her record; (2) avoiding turmoil that might make his or her job harder; and (3) how the need for his agency's personnel can be increased so he or she can rate a boost in rating and salary. It is not in the self-interest of a welfare department official to talk about reducing the number of people on welfare. He or she is likely to do everything possible to thwart that. But it might be effective to talk about new systems that will elevate the professional image of the bureaucrat handling welfare.

Judges are less susceptible to overt self-interest because they are dealing with a codified body of laws and they are subject to review by higher courts. But they are concerned that they not get publicity charging unfair or unsound judgments.

- Sympathizers—people who respond quickly to what seems to be a humanitarian, environmental, peace, or other issue.

Two main traits of Americans combine to make most people susceptible to activists' efforts: They favor the underdog against the big power, and they are always ready to grasp for an easy answer. When an activist group presents an easy answer to a problem that it says is caused by a big organization the alchemy works—most of the time. It is a challenge to the organization to inoculate the public against accepting the easy "answer" and to get people to identify their self-interest with the organization.

3. Media—which, while they sometimes present themselves as faultless oracles, are composed of people with human leanings.

Observant people were aware for years that the educational system was declining steadily in effectiveness even while costs mushroomed. But it was only when the failures of the system affected the newspapers that the press began to shout in alarm. They found that readership of newspapers was decreasing because people were coming out of schools unable or disinclined to read. And they were having more trouble finding people—even graduates of journalism schools—who can write with fundamental skill and discipline.

Similarly, crime was just something that helped sell newspapers until the kidnappings of publisher Reg Murphy and publisher's daughter Patricia Hearst and the dynamite killing of reporter Don Bolles. Then the press' call was raised for a crusade to meet the mounting crime menace.

## Reversing Negative Views

There are various instances in which the apparent self-interest of dissident groups was reversed when facts were presented in a new light.

The medical profession was losing the battle to remain free of socialization until it was shown the truth about focusing on the public's self-interest. After the 1968 passage of Medicare and Medicaid in an emotional outburst against the profession, predictions were widely made that medicine would be completely socialized within five years. Then the profession began to emphasize the effects on patients of having all doctors employed by government like postal clerks. Many people decided they didn't want their babies' delivery as unpredictably handled as their mail delivery. There is still plenty of alarm about the cost of health care and the incomes of doctors. But long before the public swung toward reducing government controls in other areas, the sentiment for government operation of health care waned.

For years the State of Illinois had a problem with the "anywhere but here" syndrome in locating a new prison. Plan after plan for its installation had to be scrapped because of local opposition. Then when the economy went sour in 1982 and unemployment was the greatest concern, the value of a prison to a local economy was stressed. Cities began to compete for the prison. When Danville was chosen there were celebrations there—and disappointment in other places.

Attacks on big government have been trumpeted since Franklin D. Roosevelt began the New Deal in 1933. Hundreds of businesses and associations ran opinion campaigns about what government regulations and controls were doing to them. It was not until the approach changed to *demonstrating* how controls raised costs and stifled the economy that people became receptive. When the time became ripe due to the stagnation of the economy, people began to recognize their self-interest in supporting deregulation.

The stranglehold of the Postal Service on delivery of all kinds of mail was impregnable until new air courier services demonstrated what could be done with packages. They helped people see the advantages to them of better handling of their written communications.

The teamsters' union joined with some major trucking companies to keep featherbedding through government controls that forbade efficient operations. When the rapid rise in prices made the public receptive to descriptions of how these controls raised costs, even extralegal efforts of the teamsters and truckers couldn't prevent decontrol.

It is wise to assess the possibility of working out an agreement with dissidents; but it is wishful thinking to believe, with Lyndon Johnson, that all differences can be worked out by "reasoning together."

For years it has been a widely held tenet that friction between groups of people is the result of separateness; that if only they could be brought together and "get to know each other" they would develop mutual respect and understanding.

That is the principle behind "involvement" and "reasoning together," both of which have many vocal adherents.

But like many "rules," it's often untrue. Few groups are more "involved" with each other or understand each other so well as the Protestants and Catholics in Northern Ireland, the Turks and Greeks on Cyprus, neighboring tribes in Nigeria, the Jews and Arabs in the Middle East, and blacks and whites in South Africa.

For leaders of organizations this means:

1. Consider interchange and involvement with all publics. Often they can lead to improved relations. But assess realistically the varied viewpoints. Which are areas where mutual interests may be furthered . . . and where is there nothing to be gained?

2. Don't let natural American optimism color judgment on group relationships. The confident sales-oriented manager feels he can sell anyone whatever he wants to sell. The reality of group dynamics argues against that possibility where groups have goals other than what appears on the surface. Judge the chances for any progress soberly and realistically.

The self-interest principle can also be applied to bolstering the resources of the organization. It is the basis for creating coalitions. Other organizations and groups can become allies when the benefits to them are made clear.

There are two types of coalition:

1. The temporary alliance working together to achieve one immediate goal over the opposition of dissidents or supporters of an opposite cause.

A major coalition of labor, business, and professional organizations fostered the 1981 reversal of tax policy that was stifling investment. There are a National Coalition of Labor Law Reform and many others that form and dissolve.

2. Permanent coalitions that work together on issues that will not be settled by one or two actions. There is a coalition of energy companies and users, Americans for Nuclear Energy; a Coalition of Independent College and University Students; an Action Committee on Technology.

While mutual self-interest can bring coalitions together, separate self-interests can sabotage their effectiveness. Shades of difference in purpose, internal politics, personal ambitions of executives—all of these and more can so clog the machinery that a coalition can be far less effective than an organization working alone.

It is vital to retain freedom to make decisions and take actions on your own if the coalition becomes paralyzed or is diverted.

# CHAPTER 11

# Using
# Effective
# Persuasion

ACTIVIST GROUPS HAVE DOMINATED MEDIA COVERAGE both
because of their own tactics and the susceptibility of media
people to their efforts.

Conditions that have loaded the deck for activists include:

- They are responsible to no one and thus need show no
  sense of responsibility.
- They have a penchant for the simplistic and the startling
  that provide just what the media want.
- A majority of media people are also anti-organization
  and so are inclined to be receptive to activists.
- Media people are not forewarned of the unsoundness of
  the activists' case and are thus inclined to accept it at face
  value.
- The media do not receive countervailing factual information in a form that is effective.

The first three of these conditions we have examined. The other two are among the conditions organizations must master to win the battle for the minds and leanings of the decision takers.

Forearming the media is part of a process of inoculation that is neglected by most organizations.

The process by which information is conveyed to people and persuades them is one of the most complex in human affairs. There are many elements that affect the process and determine whether efforts succeed or fail.

These conditions and circumstances[1] affect the readiness of the person to accept and be motivated:

1. The predisposition of the intended recipient. This is a composite of his or her heritage, outlook on life and on the subject of the communication that has accumulated through his lifetime, his fears, training, group memberships, and so on. It is preponderantly based on the self-interest of the recipient. Without that, it is unlikely that you can capture his or her interest.

2. The innate propensity to believe what is comforting to one's psyche or that shields it from guilt or fear.

3. The basic needs of the individual, such as individual worth, group acceptance, self-admiration, security, skill, knowledge, and power.

4. The basic need for harmony between the individual's needs and desires, and the social demands and pressures on him or her, including conscience and other forces. The person inherently moves toward acceptance of what enhances harmony and shields himself from what might create dissonance within him.

5. Fidelity of the message. Does it reach the recipient in the shape in which it was sent? This involves the physics of transmission—sound waves, light waves, and so on; the clarity of both transmission and reception, including such mat-

---

[1]Adapted from *Lesly's Public Relations Handbook, 3rd Edition*, edited by Philip Lesly. Prentice-Hall, Inc., Englewood Cliffs, N. J., 1983. Chapter 3.

ters as whether accents are recognizable or colors are clear;
and the semantics involved: Do sender and auditor give the
same precise meanings to words and symbols?

6. The skill and experience of the communicator—the
overriding factor in all communications efforts. Masterly
skills can work wonders; ineptness or amateurishness can
create directly opposite results. Is he or she sharply attuned
to "getting inside the skin" of the recipients, understanding
how they will receive and respond to any messages? Is he a
master at formulating and projecting messages so they will
reach the recipients under optimum circumstances and be
readily decoded into the desired form?

7. There is a wide range of what might be called susceptibility to being moved by communications. "People with low
self-esteem (i.e., those persons high in measures of social
inadequacy, inhibition of aggression, and depressive tenden-
cies) are more likely to be influenced by persuasive communications than are those with high self-esteem; but those
with acute neurotic symptoms (i.e., neurotic anxiety or obses-
sional reactions) are more likely to be resistant. Those low in
self-esteem are easily persuasible by others because they lack
character of their own; the neurotic are too disturbed, too
self-concerned, or too negativistic to pay attention or to
care."[2]

That means that the organization's communications are
unlikely to be effective with the people most likely to be a
part of, or sympathetic to, the opposing movement. In addition to avoiding giving too much attention to those who are
already strong supporters—preaching to the converted—it is
also wise to count little on influencing those who are anti-
organization because of their low esteem or neurotic tenden-
cies.

8. Among the most important variable factors deter-

---

[2]*Human Behavior*, by Bernard Berelson & Gary A. Steiner, Harcourt, Brace &
World, 1964, p. 536.

mining where communications are effective is the rapport between the source and the intended recipient.

The more trustworthy, credible, or prestigious the communicator is perceived to be, the less manipulative his intent is considered to be and the greater the immediate tendency to accept his conclusions. However, within reasonable limits, the credibility of the source has little or no influence on the transmission of factual information.

When the audience has little or no prior knowledge of the communicator's trustworthiness, it tends to decide a question on the basis of the content itself—i.e., the conformity of the content to predispositions. When the audience does expect or attribute manipulative intent . . . it develops resistance to acceptance of the message.[3]

9. As the proportion increases of people who have grown up with television as the primary influence, the whole pattern of how ideas are established has changed. People who are oriented to instant visual involvement tend to be impatient with complicated interplay between elements of society. They have less patience with "working things out." They see all problems resolved in a thirty-minute drama and all commercials assuring answers to desires. That tends to create a euphoric certainty that all things are attainable readily and quickly, and a resultant frustration when answers don't come easily, but, instead, problems grow. Communicating with these people requires graphic, action orientation.

10. The primacy of visibility determines the level of importance given to any subject. When activism against the Vietnam War was high in late 1969, America was losing about 85 men a week. At the same time, more than 1,000 people a week were lost in automobile accidents. But the war was highly visible and had been made into an emotional issue. Automobile accidents are seldom shown on TV, a camera is rarely focused on beraved relatives, a mother is not

---

[3]ibid., pp. 537-8

shown receiving a folded flag from the casket of a son who died in a smashed car. The toll in Vietnam was terrible, but it was its visibility that made it a flaming issue on the streets while the slaughter on the highways got minor attention.

In the TV age, visibility is clearly of great importance. But it is too simplistic to define "visual" as only what can be shown. Music that motivates emotion creates mental images—as the Beatles and Woodstock proved. Messages that stir emotions resulting in action become visual—as Hitler and Churchill showed.

So the principle is: What can be made to capture the imagination by becoming real forces in people's minds— actions, emotion-stirring music or speeches, films, dramatizations, events, observances, displays or symbols—has a chance to capture public support.

11. In most cases the person selects the media he or she really attends to. Appearance of a message in a medium to which he has elected to expose himself predetermines a likely disposition toward at least recognizing and considering that message.

This is increasingly a vital factor in weighing the comparative value of discretionary media exposure (editorial material in newspapers and magazines, broadcast content of TV and radio, theatrical motion pictures, books) and imposed media exposure (advertisements, TV and radio commercials, literature not requested by the recipient, commercial motion pictures, propaganda speeches). Without willing exposure by selection of the medium, many people cannot be reached by many messages, regardless of how much is spent or how massive the efforts to impose the message on them.

However, where the message is not critical to the person's psychic assurance, under certain circumstances, with massive communications efforts, it is possible to get a specific concept to take hold.

12. For communication to take place, the audience must be in what might be called a "posture of receptivity." As we have seen, the adoption of a message by its object results

from a complex combination of preconditioning influences. Aside from those that make up the character of the recipient himself, there are the many previous exposures to the source of any given message. The favorable inclination of an individual toward all messages from a given source is the result of total experience with that source. The character of the organization as exemplified by its actions, the sincerity and trustworthiness of its previous statements, the value provided in its products or services, and other influences set the stage for the enthusiasm or rejection with which the organization's communication is met.

13.  There is a "threshold of consciousness" that must be passed before an idea becomes a factor in the attitude of an individual or a group. With millions of subjects attempting to intrude upon the consciousness of each individual, the process through which a concept passes from complete obscurity through the various stages of awareness in one's mind, until at last it "is there" and an influence, is one of the great unexplored areas of psychology. There is no doubt, however, that every idea that comes to have an influence passes through the screen of resistance that the individual must erect to block out the majority of clamoring ideas seeking his attention. Whether it is one of thousands of attractive girls who somehow becomes what the public knows as Bo Derek, or a conception of social change requiring a broadening of one's horizons to encompass formerly foreign interests, it is only through a multitude of impressions coming from many directions that the threshold is crossed and the concept imbeds itself.

14.  From this we can discern that establishing an idea in the public mind calls for a "multiple-channel approach." If the idea of owning a boat is expressed a dozen times by one's teen-age son, for instance, it is quite different from having twelve different respected people, in a dozen different situations and circumstances, talk enthusiastically about the fun and excitement of boating. When a multiple combination of impressions impinges on one's attention, the impression is

created that the idea is all-pervading, that it is "the thing to do." It therefore has considerably greater influence. The same number of messages are likely to be far more effective if they are directed through many channels—newspapers, radio commentators, television programs, inclusion in motion pictures, word-of-mouth discussion, club meetings, and other channels—than repeatedly through the same means. It is no longer likely that successful communication can be confined to an organization's newspaper, or just advertisements in the local press, or any other one or two outlets.

Today we are experiencing an explosion of the scope that influencing of public opinion must cover. Besides the wire services and major newspapers, there are many more magazines, plus the multiplying forces of television, radio, motion pictures, and mass-distributed books. A majority of the population represents the public to be reached, and it is educated, diffuse, and skeptical. Except for an extremely rare occasion such as the first landing on the moon or the effort to assassinate President Reagan, no single event achieves general recognition immediately.

People must be reached by many channels, over a period of time, in the contexts of many diverse outlooks and windows on the world.

15. The more closely a communication is beamed to a specific audience or single recipient, the more likely it is to be received and accepted. "Communications directed to particular audiences are more effective than those directed to the 'public at large,'" concluded Berelson and Steiner.[4]

16. The more sharply the key point of a communication is focused for the recipient, the more likely he or she is to grasp it. At the same time, it must not be condescending or seem to insult his or her intelligence. The recipient should be led to draw the conclusion and yet not feel that his conclusions are being imposed upon him. Berelson and Steiner's research showed: "Especially on complex matters, the ex-

---

[4]ibid., p. 540

plicit drawing of conclusions by the communicator is more effective in bringing about audience acceptance than relying upon the audience to draw its own conclusions from the material presented—and presumably this is the more so the less intelligent or the less educated the audience."[5]

17. The early reaction to events may disguise their actual effects. Great publicity and furor may seem to create public opinion because of their immediacy, visibility, and force. But often there is a reaction against that furor that is more substantial and lasting. The uproar caused by the Students for a Democratic Society in 1968—especially in disrupting the Democratic convention—was aimed at grabbing public attention and radicalizing millions of young people. The tumult they created was one of the most-exposed news events in recent years. Yet studies made by the University of Michigan after the election showed that more young people had been moved to vote for right-wing candidates than had been moved to follow the SDS. Much of the public desire to "cool off" the racial issues at the start of the '70s was due to reaction against the trumpeted violence of the Black Panthers.

18. The number and types of media have expanded greatly and there is a vast range of subjects that clamor for the individual's attention. The days when a person read or at least looked at everything exposed to him are over. The individual is free to choose the communications he will expose himself to.

It is necessary to make the person's self-interest so visible, immediately, he or she feels the urge to expose the psyche to the message.

## Making Persuasive Communication Possible

Here are some guidelines that make effective communication possible:

---

[5]ibid., p. 552-3

- Approaching everything from the viewpoint of the audience's interest—what's on *their* minds, what's in it *for them*.

- Giving the audience a sense of involvement in the communication process and in what's going on. Get them involved and you get their interest.

- Making the subject matter part of the atmosphere the audience lives with—what they talk about, what they hear from others. That means getting the material adopted in *their* channels of communication.

- Communicating *with* people, not *at* them. Communication that approaches the audience as a target makes people put their defenses up against it.

- Localizing—getting the message conveyed as close to the individual's own milieu as possible.

- Using a number of channels of communication, not just one or two. The impact is far greater when it reaches people in a number of different forms.

- Maintaining consistency—so what's said on the subject is the same no matter which audience it's directed to or what the context is.

- Still, tailor-making each message for the specific audience as much as possible.

- Not propagandizing but making sure that you make your point. When a communicator draws conclusions in his summation of information, it's more effective than depending on the audience to draw its own conclusions.

- Maintaining credibility—which is essential for all of these points to be effective.

A number of trends have been changing how it is possible to communicate with the public. They make some traditional principles and methods obsolete.

1. People are less able to read. Television, educational permissiveness, and the development of graphic textbooks and other materials have all led to lessened reading ability that persists throughout life.

2. People are less willing to read. Sales of books have

not kept pace with either population or levels of education; many best sellers are quasi-books on diet, cults, anecdotes, and formulas for living. Readership of serious magazines is small and newspaper readership has been declining gradually. Most people read about a few favorite subjects.

3. People in careers—an increasing proportion of the populace—face more to read than ever. Journals and studies are numerous. In self-defense, these people avoid reading unless they have strong concern about the subject involved.

4. Solid bodies of type are the antithesis of the visual communication that most people like. A manuscript or report composed of solid type, without graphics or open space, seems to many people to be an invasion of their time and inclinations.

5. People are accustomed to having problems wrapped up neatly for them. Television shows usually end with a clear-cut conclusion. Journal articles often begin with a précis and end with a summary. People now expect to have an answer that sticks out of a manuscript like a handle they can grasp.

To communicate effectively in this climate requires that one carefully avoid discommunicating because of information overload. No matter how complex or lengthy written material must be, it can be made more persuasive through these techniques:

1. Make the case in a summary that precedes or opens the weighty matter. It should be simple, direct, and brief.

2. Summarize the key points with pithy, concise statements, itemized and preceded by bullets (•).

3. Grasp the audience's self-interest at once by ringing a bell in its mind or driving home an urgent point.

4. Use graphics if they are available and show motion to create emotion.

5. Keep it brief, with an economy of words. If a full document is needed to support the case, it can be a big ap-

pendix attached to a brief summary. Sometimes it will not be necessary to provide the full document; instead, it can be offered on request to those who really want it. That will maintain credibility provided by the full documentation but save expense in producing unneeded copies.

The Cooperative Extension Services of the United States Department of Agriculture has studied the comparative effectiveness of various forms of communication. It postulates that effectiveness of the learning process among the audience increases as it moves from *listening* to *seeing* to *doing*; that people remember about 20 percent of what they are told; 30 percent of what they see; 50 percent of what they see and hear; 70 percent of what they say; and 90 percent of what they do. It projects an ascending scale of learning effectiveness from bottom to top as follows:

- Talks and printed matter
- Charts, graphs, posters, maps, illustrated talks
- Radio, recordings, still pictures
- Slides, film strips
- Movies, TV, theatricals
- Exhibits, displays
- Field trips, tours
- Demonstrations
- Discussions
- Contests, judging
- Participation in dramatics
- Working with models, games
- Actual experience, projects

This type of generalized guide is helpful but, like all aspects of communication, varies greatly according to subject, timing, nature of the audiences, and other factors.

## Key Elements for Effectiveness

It is vital to keep clear the difference between *persuading* someone and *convincing* him or her.

*Persuasion* is getting the person to do something. *Convincing* is getting a point of view firmly accepted. You can convince someone but not persuade him or her—if no action results. One of the most common errors in the English language today is misuse of these words—and that leads to .many errors in communication. It is incorrect to say, "I convinced him to go to the game with me today." It is also an error to believe that if you have convinced someone of your point of view you have gained an ally who will act for you.

On the other hand, remember that in most cases all that is necessary for an organization is to defuse the audience's penchant for pursuing a viewpoint just because its only input comes from the opposition. If you can fill that vacuum and balance the pros and cons in the audience's mind—even if you don't convince them that you are right—you can neutralize the opponents' impact. You don't have to make them your allies, only prevent them from being your opponents' allies.

So there are three distinct stages that your communication can cover:

- Neutralization
- Conviction
- Persuasion

To bring the audience to these three stages requires masterly knowledge and skills in the techniques of *communication especially suited to the conditions and challenges of this age of activism*.

The tactics of activists can be thwarted with techniques of the 1980s rather than weighty word-oriented techniques. The principles for winning a communication battle involve:

- *Simplicity.* The message must be understood easily and immediately by an unsophisticated audience that has an aversion to scientific information. That includes media.

- *Clarity.* It must be sharp and not subject to vagueness or any alternative meanings.

- *Brevity.* Most people today—including media people— don't like to read anything but their favorite subjects. They are turned off by heavy, difficult, or lengthy reading material. Almost all magazines requiring careful thought are gone. Even newspaper readership is decreasing gradually. To get people to read today it is *essential* to lure them by making it obviously easy, to do their work for them by condensing information and ideas into minimum space, to give them a sense of having done a great task while they're actually doing only a little work.

    Solid scholarly documents are needed to provide proof that the support is there for the "headline" treatments. But do not expect that lengthy documents will be read, understood, and analyzed intelligently.

- *Impact.* Material must be striking or stirring, which brings with it the emotion that must accompany facts. The material should grab the audience's attention in some legitimate manner. It should make a striking statement, startle the senses, or otherwise break through the wall of resistance the person has around his or her psyche.

- *Visualization.* In an age of TV and film, people— including Congressmen and heads of agencies—are moved primarily by facts or events that create images in their minds. That means not only using photos or film when possible, but also other means of creating those mental images—examples, metaphors, parables, anecdotes, and the like. (See Chapter 19.)

# SECTION FOUR

# Tactics

# CHAPTER 12

# Don't Give Ammunition to Your Enemies

IN MOST CASES ACTIVISTS ARE SHORT ON EVERYTHING except passion. They not only are short of money, management skills, and manpower, they probably are short of facts and logic to support their cause. If they have facts and logic, in today's litigious system they are likely to go directly to the courts and bypass other confrontations.

They are short of ammunition to wage their battle—so they count on you to provide it.

Countless confrontations have been fueled with ammunition provided by the organization that was being attacked. Here are basic rules for avoiding being maneuvered into providing the opponents' ammunition:

1. Review what your organization does that might be made to seem abusive in the hands of emotion-wringing opponents. Does the membership or employment application

seem to put some people at a disadvantage? Is local traffic tied up at your rush hours, and could they be staggered?

2. Don't be cast into the role of a bully. Jerry Rubin, one of the most articulate of the 1960s activists, said: "A movement cannot grow without repression." So don't plant spies in the opponents' camp. (That doesn't prevent open observation and review of their actions and statements.)

3. Don't threaten or browbeat. The organization has the role of the big, powerful institution. The opponents cast themselves as the oppressed. Consider how every action you take will *seem to be* or *be made to appear by vocal activists*—and avoid whatever can be cast as bullying.

4. Ridicule can be a devastating tool for deflating puffed up charges—but it can also blow up in your face. If efforts to ridicule your opponents work, they can be made to seem ridiculous and fade away. But if your efforts are not sharp and devastating, they can create acrimony that will boost the opponents' supporters and make your organization seem to be ham-handed.

The best way to make them seem ridiculous is to let their own actions or words do it. A calm, precise point-by-point rebuttal of a list of activists' charges, for instance, can deflate observers' respect for their case.

5. Watch very carefully your reactions to what your opponents do or say. *Many of their initiatives are designed to evoke responses from you that will give them ammunition.* Their tenet is: "The real action is the enemy's reaction."

General Motors' reaction to Ralph Nader's little-known book catapulted him and his causes into a long period of potency. The reaction of the Chicago police to the Yippies at the 1968 Democratic convention made major issues of their previously ineffective charges. The reaction of southern sheriffs, in using police dogs and water hoses, made martyrs of black marchers who previously got little attention.

Before you react, think of what they're trying to evoke; what media and public reaction may be; and what response you can make that will deny them what they're seeking.

6. Avoid name-calling. They may use epithets, but if you do—"anarchists," "communists," "fuzzy-minded radicals who want to destroy our system"—you come off as a bully who can't respond to charges with substantive answers.

7. Disarm their efforts to make you look bad. If they make loud demands for a meeting, in the expectation your leaders will be too busy to spend their time on futile discussion, consider inviting them into a comfortable conference room, assigning officials as a committee speaking for your organization, and inviting the media. If they rant and rave, let them. If they try to argue on the basis of logic and fact, you should prevail if you are properly prepared and the merits are on your side.

8. Don't have opponents jailed unless it's clearly in the *public's* interest. Jailing focuses attention on the power of the opposition's leaders: They must be real threats if the target organization thinks it has to have them jailed. It solidifies the supporters of the cause: The leader is made to seem dedicated and his cause just if he's ready to go to jail.

However, when it's apparent that the public will support having legal action taken, it can be considered. When a supporter of the Equal Rights Amendment was convicted of trying to bribe a state legislator, only her closest supporters demurred. When others marred the priceless marble floor of the state legislature with blood, their jailing got widespread public support.

9. The most potent ammunition an activist group can have is the promise that its expectations will be fulfilled. That's why in rallies and exhortations activist leaders hold out "victory" as just within reach. It inspires followers to maintain the pressure. And if victory is denied, the reaction can be a stimulus to heightened effort. "A grievance is most poignant when almost redressed," Eric Hoffer said. So don't help build up expectations that are not going to be fulfilled. If a compromise or settlement will be made, let it be better than anything the opponents were led to expect from you until the end.

10. Don't stiffen their resistance by making them feel betrayed or put upon. Avoid what can be twisted into being called double-dealing or Indian giving.

11. Do your homework. Carl Gerstacker, former Chairman of Dow Chemical Company, advises: ". . . know . . . your position so thoroughly that you deal from a position of overwhelming strength and being so confident in this strength that you can deal with the protesters with a maximum of patience, diplomacy and grace. . . . Don't ever be afraid to over-prepare for a confrontation situation. . . . You may be outraged, and much of the time you should be, by (their) behavior, but the first and most important thing of all is to keep your cool, in spite of their efforts."

12. Don't insist on "winning." Aim for a situation in which the opponents can also claim they accomplished a goal. They need to save face. Both Orientals, who put high value on face, and most activists are oriented most to emotions and appearances. If their emotion and sense of dignity are assuaged, they may retire to other frays with no lasting enmity against you.

# CHAPTER 13

# Opponents Need Conflict

LEADERS OF ORGANIZATIONS TEND TO BE BOLD MEN OF AC-
TION. By instinct and training they are averse to accepting
abuse without making a sharp response. So they are inclined
to fight back.

In overcoming opposition, however, there is an important difference between decisiveness and fighting.

Conflict is often exactly what the opponents seek—what
they need not only to achieve their goals, but even to hold
their supporters together. By turning provocations into conflict, organizations often provide their enemies with precisely
what they want most.

Alinsky said: "The cessation of action brings death to an
organization (of activists) through factionalism and inaction."

To activists there are three kinds of action:

1. Initiatives that attract attention to their cause.
2. Actual developments that bring about their goals.

3. Actions that engage the opposition and thereby provide the milieu the activists need.

Conflict affords a number of benefits to activist groups:

● It provides provocative rhetoric and fulfills the romantic fantasies that many disenchanted people seek to instill excitement into their lives.

● It is probably the most certain means of creating news and making the group seem to be important.

● It seems to demonstrate the vitality of the movement. Conflict is action, and action creates the image of virility.

● It seems to prove the existence of a devil that the movement confronts and must overcome. Eric Hoffer said: "A mass movement can rise and spread without belief in a God, but never without belief in a devil."

● It creates a sense of crisis and a threat that not only rallies existing members of the movement, but tends to rush others into alliances for "mutual defense" against "repression."

Jerry Rubin said:

> Repression turns demonstration protests into wars. Actors into heroes. Masses of individuals into a community. Repression eliminates the bystander, the neutral observer, the theorist. It forces everyone to pick a side.

● It is a means of letting the world know that the movement is alive. Particularly for underground movements, conflict is a form of communication. The FALN that wants to have Puerto Rico cut loose from the United States does it with bombs. The Weathermen, in their "Days of Rage," did it by breaking windows and destroying property. Efforts of law enforcement people to capture the culprits further publicized the existence of the groups. Activist groups have been known to sacrifice members in conflict so they would become "martyrs" and symbols.

The literalness of conflict as communication for the

movement is given book-length treatment in *Violence As Communication*, by Alex P. Schmid and Jonny de Graaf.

• Conflict becomes a tool in rivalries between activist and terrorist groups. And it creates a chain reaction of imitation. "These things feed on each other," an FBI specialist is quoted in *Newsweek*. "They hate to be upstaged."

Many activist groups have protested in rage that their acts have not evoked publicity-creating response, while the PLO and other terrorist groups are played up in media all over the world.

Conflict is also useful for people in government. By demonstrating that there is a devil out there they can justify their existence and need for increased budgets.

Many Congressional and administrative hearings are called solely to present "servants of the people" in the role of gladiators taking on some organizational monster.

A government bureau endangered with withering apathy will seek to provoke a belligerent response to its proposed rulings: That lifts an administrative report into an exciting joust, with the bureaucrats in the role of gladiator. Output of American farms greatly exceeds demand and more soil is going into crop production than the small amount lost to erosion in a few areas; but the United States Soil Conservation Service issues alarming reports about a "crisis" impending because of erosion. It hopes to make the subject a raging controversy, which naturally would require it to hire more "experts" to prove its case.

## How to Avoid Playing into Their Hands

Great sensitivity and judgment are required to resist the machinations of opponents without giving them the conflict they may be seeking.

Some of the principles for achieving this are covered in chapters that follow. Meanwhile, here are some guiding principles for developing strategy when confronted with opposition that may be trying to provoke conflict:

● Remember that in America, all excesses create their own demise. The Black Panthers and the Weather Underground destroyed their public support by going too far in their aggressions. Americans are a people of moderation. Extremists of all kinds lose public sympathy. One of the most visible forces for reducing public support for welfare was the aggressiveness of some welfare mothers in demanding more handouts to support their various fatherless children.

David Dellinger of the "Chicago Seven" acknowledged that:

> ... if street fighting breaks out when the police are restrained and if we act contemptuously of people's rights, the sentiments of those who should be our allies could turn against us.

● Require that decision-makers give careful study to the issue—making it subject to scientific and other review. Raise the issue out of the streets and into the forum of reasoned judgment. To do that requires the techniques of getting sound and thorough information into the channels through which judgments will be formed. Be seen as the reasoned and reasonable party; let your opponents depict themselves as the rash and unreasoned.

● If the opponents' case lacks merit, there need be nothing inevitable about the changes they demand. If the issue is seen to be complex and have no simple answer, the great majority of people will refuse to make up their minds (unless the subject is of direct concern to them). Having the issue considered carefully slows down the process from headlong to reasoned. Then change delayed can be change prevented.

# CHAPTER 14

# Opponents Need Victories

$F$EW MOVEMENTS CAN WITHSTAND THE BOREDOM of dull debates and waiting for decisions. Except when intolerable personal problems are involved—such as being drafted to fight in Vietnam or having their children bused into slum neighborhoods—people who support movements need periodic stimulus to keep their enthusiasm. Since the great majority of these people have few victories in their lives (people who do are usually too busy and too self-integrated to pursue causes that do not involve their expertness or interests) the hunger for "achievement" is a lure, and its absence turns them off.

When the "infant formula problem" was being trumpeted in the media and the World Health Organization passed a code that supposedly would assure safe feeding of babies all over the world, many supporters of the cause proudly told their friends how they had helped save millions of babies' lives.

A victory for most activist groups is not like a victory in the Olympics, after which the laurel bearer goes home to applause and retirement. It is more like a victory in a baseball season, when there are many more contests to go. The headiness of victory is usually not turned off; it is a stimulus to press for more victories.

Sy Kahn in *Organizing* has this advice for movement leaders:

> As a leader you want to encourage people to keep their vision open-ended. Don't let people say, "I'll be glad when this is over because then we won't have to meet anymore." Help them feel, "If we win this one, we're going to have the strength to go on to the next one."

Conservationists won the right to *conserve* natural resources so they would be used prudently and perpetuated for permanent use. But that was taken over by many environmentalists, who demand that natural resources not be used at all; that the millions of square miles of the United States owned by the government be absolutely barred from cultivation of their resources—both renewable, such as timber, and non-renewable but essential, such as oil and minerals that now must be imported at great cost in unemployment and high prices.

Pressure groups that started by calling for giving everyone equal opportunity gained that worthy goal. But they moved on to demand that everyone be guaranteed equal success—automatic guarantees of executive jobs, guarantees of getting a college degree, and the like.

Labor groups, seeking to assure that wages would keep up with inflation—caused partially by raising wages—demanded cost-of-living formulas. That concept was quickly adopted by government employees, retirees on Social Security, and others. That victory won—greatly reducing the possibility of holding down inflation without creating unemployment—the pressure groups went on to demand increases *greater* than the rise in inflation. That gave them an incentive for helping increase inflation.

The importance of getting victories at regular intervals was well-recognized by Alinsky:

"Sometimes the organizer may find such despair among the people that he has to put on a cinch fight."

He had neighborhood groups demand such things as extra benches or a new slide in a playground. Clearly, the group did not disperse when the benches or slide were added.

It is an irony of activism that what seems unfavorable in other contexts is good for the activists. Having someone become a martyr—preferably not fatally—can be treated as a victory, in addition to providing the climate of conflict they seek. Local celebrities of a few weeks have been created by being arrested for lying down before a bulldozer at a power plant construction site.

Victories also contribute to the momentum of activists' growth—the bandwagon effect. People—especially those who know few achievements in their lives—are readily recruited.

Leaders of the activist movement take on the aura of heroes, in an age when the constant spotlight of electronic media does far more to debunk heroism than to create it.

Coalitions are more easily formed by a group that can trumpet its victories. Other groups, themselves hungry for some sign of success, may temporarily give up focusing on their specific causes and join what looks like a wedge to gain some footing.

When the WHO passed its code on infant formulas, various groups that had started with other interests joined, for a time, the infant formula movement. (The lesson came later. When most of the movement's case was deflated by scrupulous and effective examination of the facts, the coalition ceased to be a source of victories. Various groups moved on to pursue their special interests.)

When the Proposition 13 referendum was passed in California, greatly reducing property taxes, the bandwagon effect became evident. Other groups joined the original Jarvis-Gann organization, and similar movements arose in many other parts of the country, not only fighting for tax-reduction referenda, but for other causes that legislators were not acting on.

On the other hand, when victories fail to come, not only do a group's supporters fall away, its credibility is weakened. For the groups that organized to fight inflation by picketing supermarkets—comparable to attacking the scales for showing an increase in one's weight—victories were not forthcoming. In most cases the leaders of those demonstrations were not so able to arouse emotions on behalf of the next cause they undertook.

### Establishing a Strategy

As in many other aspects of overcoming opposition, there is a narrow line between withholding victories and coming across as intransigent. One of the goals of activists is to depict the target organization as unreasonable and unwilling to hold reasonable negotiations.

Judgment calls for avoiding having the opposition go away with claims of victory. If possible, the conclusion at each stage should be a win/win position, with both sides able to claim a favorable result.

To achieve that, the strategy calls for this approach:

● Force the use of orderly procedures rather than decisions made under duress and in a hurry. Have ready in organized form the facts, the arguments, and the consequences of meeting the demands. Get them reviewed by the responsible and thoughtful elements of the publics involved. Use the available channels to have them discussed and considered.

● Avoid haste. Go through all the steps available to

you—discussions, review by responsible and objective organizations, drafting of proposals, development of counterproposals. Make sure that the heat of passion is not the main force behind a decision; studied consideration tends to temper passions. But don't leave yourself open to credible charges of being dilatory or dragging the matter to death.

This process of going through a schedule of procedures also has the advantage of sifting the opposition group down to its bedrock advocates.

• To achieve a win/win situation, make any concessions contingent on gaining concessions. If a neighborhood group demands a new playground, make its leaders responsible for maintaining it in usable condition. If it is damaged, that will be a major support for your cause in meeting the next demands.

• If you work out an agreement, consider the leaders of the opposition group as potential members of your team. If they impressed you as sincere and reasonable people, suggest they join you to work for mutual goals. You will gain capable people. They will gain a means to fulfill their desire for chances to accomplish things. And they will no longer be rallying points for the group to go on unilaterally grasping for more.

That process is not co-opting the opposition. It is the age-old process of absorbing the best of a rising group into the social pyramid. The process refreshes every system. It assures that the structure's arteries don't harden. And it provides a wholesome process for combining the best elements into the system where they can ferment new approaches and you can distill out the best.

# CHAPTER 15

# Opponents Often Are "Anti's"

IT IS EVIDENT FROM THE VARIOUS LOOKS we've had at the nature of opponents that it's vital to understand what makes them tick.

Whenever one deals with people there is a wide range of variations to consider and a constant degree of mystery. Nothing is more certain than that all human relations are filled with uncertainty.

While it is helpful to identify basic types of personality, it is a mistake to assume that all people will rigidly follow any group of profiles.

The categories of opponents cited in Chapter 4 (advocates, dissidents, activists, and zealots) are helpful in understanding the need for careful selection of approaches. Even those categories, however, do not cover all the variations. For instance, there is a class of zealots that may be called fanatics, some of whom blow up children and hijack airplanes.

Another requirement is analyzing the fundamental motivation of people in opposition groups—to probe their psyches and understand what brings them into this particular cause at this specific time.

Again, classifying them by types is a useful aid to organized thinking; but it is important to recognize that the lines between the groups are not sharp and that the groups do not include all shades of motivation.

Most of them can be described as being one of these five types:

1. Sincere people with a clear purpose that frankly reflects their rights or interests.

2. Do-gooders who are comfortable and usually affluent. They seek an outlet for their purposefulness in helping others or in making things fit their theories of life.

3. Social engineers who consider themselves intellectually and morally the cream of society and are intent on imposing their superior judgment onto the entire human system.

4. The holier-than-thou who feel that heaven has anointed them with the one true formula for human existence and that it is their duty to heaven to impose it on everyone else.

5. "Anti's," who are against almost everything, constantly dissatisfied with their lives and the world. They are usually unsettled in their private lives, dissatisfied or disgruntled in their working lives, and disruptive in the causes they identify with, even while they proclaim their devotion to them.

This grouping makes it clear that no single approach can satisfy the urgings of the spectrum of opponents.

Many activist groups are made up of several of these types. For example, the anti-nuclear energy movememt comprises many who are in groups 1, 2, and 4. In addition, individuals of the various types join in alliances on some issues and can be antagonists on others. Many social engineers, for instance, are strongly in favor of abortion while many holier-than-thous are strongly opposed. Yet they were aligned for a long time in the fight to give control of infant feeding to non-medical bureaucrats.

So it is important not only to understand the psyches of the people who seem to be forming an opposition to the organization; their shifting alliances can be surprising if insufficient analysis is made of how they rationalize their arguments. The anti-formula coalition in 1981 included aggressive feminists who usually feel that government should not have any say about their bodies or their family lives, and fervent anti-abortionists who were demanding that the government prevent women from having control over their sex lives and reproduction. They joined to write impassioned literature and exhort Congress. Causes make strange bedfellows, but separation is probable when the cause fades or is resolved.

A distinction should be made between the leaders and followers of various movements. The numbers of followers are usually far too great for any organization to keep track of them. And there tends to be a distinct difference in personality and approach between those who spearhead movements and those who join them.

Accordingly, while it's useful to observe the traits and impulses of the whole group, it is on the leaders that concentration must be focused.

## Understanding Motivations

A deeper look at the basic types can provide an understanding of how to deal with them.

● *Sincere people who have a legitimate interest in the issue*
Chapter 6 dealt with the purposes and nature of such people. The majority of issues that will confront an organization usually involve such people and their normal concerns:

safety of their neighborhoods, welfare of their children, security, quality of products or services, and the like. This type and its concerns are so common that they make up the usual pattern of dealings that most organizations have.

● *Do-gooders*

These people are active on matters they believe will benefit others and they have time, resources, and energy left over from attending to their affairs. They tend to be affluent and established, with little need to work hard at advancing their own careers. They often have considerable influence in their communities because of their status and their associations with other influential people. Since they seem to be selfless in pursuing "worthy causes," they usually are honored, have clout in the political arena, and are highly regarded by the media.

They start with what they think things *should* be and then look for something or someone to blame because they are not that way. They are strongly motivated to put such things right, and will not be turned away by the fact that the causes may be very complex and have no single root. They are simplifiers, black-and-white in their evaluations, and certain that they have *the* answers.

Others in this group fit the aphorism of Eric Hoffer:

"A man is likely to mind his own business when it is worth minding. When it is not, he takes his mind off his own meaningless affairs by minding other people's business."

● *Social engineers*

These are others who feel they have the answers that the mass of inferior beings must accept, but they usually have no justification—such as claimed appointment by God—except their own superiority. They are "The Best and the Brightest" of the sort who got us into Vietnam and established thousands of giveaway programs that led to America's impoverished economy that impoverished those who were supposed to be benefited.

Even more than many theologians, social engineers

carry hatred for a system that leaves the workings to those who want to do the work, rather than following the dictates of those who sit in bureaucracies and ivory towers. They are not inclined toward organizational functioning and scorn those who are, including the administrators of their universities, newspapers, social agencies, networks, and foundations. They thwart the functions needed for operation, but reject any effort to give them assignments in those functions.

They are intellects scorned, and their fury is often as hot as a woman scorned.

Machiavelli was the apotheosis of the social engineer, but he was resigned to being a courtier to the prince who had to administer his country. Today's social engineer is seldom resigned to providing advice while letting the administrator make the decisions.

● *The holier-than-thous*

Among them are theologians. Being in their own eyes the best people, and yet not being given the greatest rewards, they judge on subjective and circumstantial evidence that the world is all wrong.

A study by the Roper Center in late 1981 and early 1982 polled 1,112 professors in Christian seminaries and schools of religion. They found that 50 percent claim to be liberal, compared with 21 percent of the general public; 22 percent said they were moderates compared with 33 percent; and only 27 percent conservative as compared with 47 percent of the public. In this context, liberalism translates into motivation to restructure society to one's own specifications and conservatism to an inclination to let the system function with few restraints.

*The Christian Century* noted that activism among theologians was moving strongly in opposite directions in the name of Christ. The left-inclined activism of the National Council of Churches and leaders of some denominations was being opposed by the right-leaning activism of the Moral Majority and other aggressive fundamentalists. Both insisted that they knew what was wrong with the world, in Christ's cause, and that they were the ones to write the prescription and enforce the regimen.

● *"Anti's"*

These are the most neurotic, often including people who also fall into another category. They are people who are trapped in place while the world changes rapidly. If they could, they would scream: "Stop the world! I want to get off," but the world won't stop so they fall back on criticizing almost everything about it.

Their psyche includes resentment of those who earn more, get more excitement, enjoy life, get recognition. Since they believe that people who head organizations get all those benefits, they resent the organizations and their leaders.

They have low self-esteem and want desperately to get outside themselves, to divert their focus from their own lives to other forces. They are moved by a constant hope for early success. In fact, often it is impatience for success that under-lies their own failures: They lack the discipline and will to do what's needed and to stay on course.

They blame their failures on the strictures laid down by the system, but the last thing they want is a system in which everyone would be free to compete on the basis of merit, for they know they would lose again.

The nature of the "anti's" gives the organization they oppose a natural advantage. A high proportion of people who become activists are neurotics who constantly find fault and do not adjust well to living and working with others. They are likely to become dissatisfied with any movement they join, once the first flush of a new cause has faded. Ac-tivists tend to split off from their original groups. As discus-sions are held they find reasons to disagree. And rather than work out adjustments, they break away. They lack the sense of compromise that successful life in a complex society or any complex group requires. That's why all major movements of recent years have split up into rival and often jealous groups.

When there are successes for the movement, when they are provided with martyrdom or other annealing forces, the groups may hold the "anti's." But when they encounter difficulties—when one or more of the leaders is discredited, or their assertions are turned back on them, or ego creates friction—they begin to criticize within the movement, tempers flare, and defections occur.

Chapter 21 explores the strategies for dealing with these conditions.

# CHAPTER 16

# Don't Let Them Focus on a Single Segment

Activist groups have a great advantage because they share a major trait with the public at large: a propensity to grasp one element and believe that it is the problem or the answer to a problem. They have a simple-minded approach to a complex world which almost always has many factors intertwined.

Activists and people in general see the universe through a magnifying glass rather than a telescope.

This trait explains the intensity of single-purpose groups that are transforming the political and social fabric of the country. "Gray panthers" *know* that the main thing that must be attended to is increasing payments to Social Security holders. They vote for candidates whose other principles would lead to dissolution of the country, so long as they assert loudly enough their support for bigger Social Security funds.

The same applies to single-purpose blocs behind women's claims, blacks' advantages, pristine wilderness, and many others.

The readiness of people to accept easy answers is evident in many of the pillars of their thinking:

● *Superstitions.* Millions of people who would be insulted if you asked whether they believed bad luck was due to black cats or walking under a ladder follow the superstitions of the "enlightened" 1980s. They wear religious amulets on chains and in their cars to ward off accidents. They try to get an edge in the battle against diseases by turning to brass bracelets and then Ankh emblems. They call on divine intervention for an advantage over competitors in a ball game or to forestall rain on their wedding day. Somewhere, they are sure, among the endless succession of beauty aids and fragrances is the potion that will attract the handsome millionaire or passionate Venus.

● *Prejudices.* Easy identification of one's failures can be made not only among the familiar scapegoats identified by color or race, but from some other city, say, or among bucolic rural residents. People who get their livelihood from "nonprofit" organizations are, of course, more wholesome than those working for a corporation; religious figures are certainly gifted with higher morals than those who hold their faiths privately. Men (or women) are responsible for the breakdown of (choose): the family, moral standards, child behavior, education, the economy, the automobile accident rate, or sobriety.

● *Cults and causes.* The hunger for one-dimensional answers—and their rapid disillusion rate—can be seen through a partial rundown of those swallowed by millions within a few years, as we saw in Chapter 2. In addition, the flowering of offbeat religious cults, slowed by Jonestown, has outpaced the traditional religions whose answers were formed in simpler times.

• *Cures and health promises.* What is supposed to be the best-educated people in history—supposedly taught about the immense complexity of the human body—persists in seeking simple paths to illness-free eternity. Besides the disease-thwarting amulets, they give their faith to an endless string of diets to lose or gain weight; various one-element regimens—water, honey, organic food; fending off cancer by having spinal bones pushed around; preventing or curing hangovers without cutting down on alcohol; ginseng and other potions to increase sexual potency; curing illnesses from indigestion to obesity either through celibacy or limitless sex; salves and lotions to restore hair or to remove it.

So it is in keeping with the simple-mindedness seen in other areas that activists zero in on one element of vastly complex problems.

## Selecting "Problems"

The problem of the environment encompasses all the plants, animals, winds, storms, streams, earthquakes, and other forces over the entire globe and even in the rest of the universe. Obviously that is a very complex affair. So those who concern themselves with the state of the environment ignore all of them—and the five billion people whose natural wastes and breathing produce monstrous amounts of pollutants—to zero in on one: industrialization. They ignore the fact that pollution was much worse in inhabited areas when all houses belched out coal smoke, horses fouled all roads, garbage was dumped outdoors, and human wastes went directly through privies to the ground. They assert that the environment is now perilously poisoned and that we must stop completely all the advances that have made life bearable for more than one percent of the people.

The fact is that most pollutants are exuded by nature and people. But doing much about those sources is too formidable a task—and would interfere with what the activists themselves foster (they drive cars to their protest rallies, after all, and find chemical toilets a nuisance). So they zero in on industry—which happens to be the only means for helping the vast majority of people to improve their lives to approach the level enjoyed by the environmentalists.

The trick of focusing on one element has been developed to a fine art. Extremists among environmentalists rush to "protect" a single species as their means of blocking any development, from a dam to a tract of sorely needed new homes. They rush to defend the snail darter and the liverwort—two among an estimated 250 million species of animal life. Even in this game, enterprise will arise. Robert Zappaolorti formed a firm—himself, working out of his home—that charges $10,000 for two or three weeks' search around construction sites. He finds some form of life that the local community group can say would be endangered if a new project goes forward. One group on Long Island even held up a project in defense of an endangered microbe.

At about the age of four almost everyone discovers that the economy is imperfect: One can't get all the candy and toys one would like to have because there isn't enough money. Most people mature enough to recognize that the worldwide economic system is highly complex and can never be made perfect enough to provide everything everyone ever wants. Most of us go to work to earn enough to approach our reasonable desires. But others find the existence of imperfections intolerable and look for "the answer." The fact that the answer they find doesn't work seldom deters them, as evidenced by the repeated elections of Socialists even though no truly socialist economy has ever functioned for long except by force.

Now we see activists proposing various simple answers to the existence of poor people amongst us. To them, the existence of someone they define as poor is proof of the need to rejigger the entire economic system—even though there has never been a society without an underlayer of poor people who are inherently unable to cope with life. This underclass—which includes drifters, whores, thieves, the feckless, the inveterate lummoxes, the Jukes and the Kallikaks—has never been less than about six percent of the populace. Every society has recognized them, has borne them as the motes in their midst. Every society has discouraged their propagation—until ours.

Activists now rally around one of several simple answers—force employers to hire the underclass at good wages and promote them to managerial roles so they won't feel slighted; get them through college even if they don't learn to read or bother to attend class; put them on school boards so their children will be represented in decisions on education.

Others see that there are people who get sick, as though that were a new phenomenon. The death rate has fallen sharply. Life expectancy has shot up from 40 years to more than 73 in just the past half-century. Many diseases have been eradicated or made uncommon. Childhood illnesses have been so reduced that the most common cause of young deaths is accidents.

But still, people do get sick; so activists ignore the facts that most illnesses are primarily due to (1) people's susceptibilities at birth; and (2) their own poor habits of diet, hygiene, abstinence, and other care. They have to have something easy to grab onto, so they find there is a sewage dump somewhere, or pollutants were emitted in workplaces 30 years ago, or there is a power plant nearby. The implication, of course, is that if none of those had existed no one would ever have gotten sick.

Whenever a television show wants to cry alarm about holding down budgets it finds one or two of those people in the underclass and shows them in poverty—as though there had never been poverty before or during the years when the federal budget to help the poor was multiplying. Singling out a few instances is so much easier and more graphic than understanding the whole complex economic system.

Unemployment is high while hundreds of thousands of jobs go unfilled because they require either special skills or willingness to work as servants. Ignoring the massive problems of people's unwillingness or inability to learn the skills, or of their reluctance to do "menial work," labor activists push the easy answer: Pump taxpayers' money into highly overpaid jobs in dying industries or keep those jobs by making everything imported cost much more.

It is estimated (by highly unreliable global activists) that 10 million babies die each year throughout the world. Objective observers can readily discern that the great majority of them enter life in backward lands with archaic political structures, inhuman social structures, impoverished economies, hostile climates, unavailability of clean water, massive ignorance, widespread indolence, no transportation, hosts of insects, ill-nourished mothers, and non-existent health care facilities. Truly an overwhelming array of obstacles to an infant's survival! What do those who seek an answer grasp onto? All the factors mentioned are formidable and would require tremendous effort and resources. No, they say, let's keep all those 10 million babies alive by—banning infant formula!

We saw how the global bureaucrats use this isolation technique to press for control over the world's information, oceanic resources, economy, and health care. By isolating attention on one of their seemingly benign proposals at a time, they take the world's eye off the worldwide control that is their real goal.

It is no coincidence that almost all the social engineering programs of the past 50 years—from forced school desegregation to guaranteeing a place in college for almost everyone—have aggravated the problems they were supposed to alleviate. They all seek to solve massively complicated problems by focusing on single apparent solutions. This record of failures and all other evidence that simplistic approaches are wrong does not protect an organization from being assaulted with a simplistic attack.

Forestalling and fending off such attacks requires preventing opponents from isolating their simple answer and getting all attention focused on it.

It is necessary to *prevent* such tactics by feeding the springs of information in advance with the full facts about the complex problem—simply told and displayed.

And it is necessary to *thwart* such efforts by constantly putting opponents' simplistic charges into their full context. They will try to put limits on what is said, to concentrate on their isolated point. By constantly showing the small role it plays in the full context, you not only weaken their case but raise the doubts of the audience by filling the vacuum that makes it comfortable to form a judgment.

# CHAPTER 17

# Activists
# Love
# Vacuums

P EOPLE'S TENDENCY TO WANT SIMPLE THINGS plays into the hands of activists in another important way: By making simple assertions about the subject they often preempt the public's thinking about it. When there is a vacuum of information, the simple accusation or slogan stands alone in consideration of the issue.

That has the effect of transforming an assertion into the "information" on the subject. The public mind grasps it like a frog snapping up a fly—and slams shut.

Alinsky said: "Men will act when they are convinced their cause is 100 percent on the side of the angels and that the opposition are 100 percent on the side of the devil."

When opponents fill information vacuums with their simplistic assertions, the lazy-minded audience feels it has everything important on the subject.

The longer the vacuum of information is filled only by

such simplistic "answers," the more they are likely to seep into people's consciousness and become imbedded. The effectiveness of organizations in balancing the information is in inverse ratio to the time elapsing after opponents make their simplistic points.

Here the lazy-mindedness of the public can become an advantage for the organization. While people are comfortable accepting an isolated assertion or slogan as revealed truth, they are uncomfortable if there is conflicting information that must be weighed and evaluated. Public opinion pollsters find that on some subjects many people either express no opinion or just give one off the top of their heads to avoid seeming ignorant.

For instance, on the question of whether what children watch on television contributes to the growing rate of violence, there has been a running battle of conflicting information. As a result, many people shrug and refuse to take sides. Murmurs about the extent of violence on TV continue, but little action has been imposed on broadcasters.

Similarly, there has been substantial information on both sides of the question of whether generic drugs are as dependable as those carrying the brand names of the producers. The drug industry has drawn on the work of thousands of highly qualified experts in a field in which the public knows it lacks expertness. It has kept the populace neutral by neutralizing activists' assertions.

So the primary strategy in forestalling opponents' efforts is to fill the information vacuum. Nature abhors vacuums but activists love them.

A look at some of the causes propounded by activist groups indicates how readily they have made progress in fostering spurious positions because those who know most about the subject have neglected this strategy:

- "We couldn't get our menial work done without illegal aliens."
- "Society—not criminals—is responsible for crime."

- "Prisons don't reduce crime" (although 85 percent of all listed crimes are committed by repeaters).
- "The poor educational achievement of children is due to inadequate spending."
- "Millions of the elderly will starve if Social Security payments are not constantly increased."
- "Social Security is a sacred commitment to repay people what they have paid into the fund."
- "America is a wealthy society so everyone is entitled to a high standard of living."
- "The wealthy in America don't pay taxes."
- "People in poor neighborhoods don't get the services their taxes pay for."
- "Slums create poverty."
- "Americans' eating habits are causing millions of people in underdeveloped countries to starve."

That emphasizes again this vital strategy:

- Do homework in advance on any subject that may become the basis of an activist crusade.
- Prepare the most authoritative, objective, convincing documentation on all aspects of the subject.
- Prepare it in a way that appeals to the audience's desire for simplicity—short summaries of key points set off with marks—• and ¶; condensed highlight sheets to which the full document becomes the appendix of support material; graphics—charts, illustrations, graphs; white space that makes the material both inviting and simple-looking.
- Make this authoritative material part of the consideration process on the subject as early as possible—while opinions are being shaped rather than after the opponents' simplistic assertions have taken root.
- Use the most sophisticated methods of disseminating information (see Chapter 11).
- Meet every thrust by opponents with the full scope of facts—without taking a defensive posture. Sound, au-

thoritative, objective information presented in an unargumentative tone is usually the best antidote.

- Constantly expose new facts or events that contradict the opponents' simplistic case. Work on their greatest vulnerability—loss of the respect and support of fair-minded people among thought leaders.

- Make it clear that the opposition will constantly be entangled in justifying its position against facts and logic: Be the porcupine instead of the lamb.

# CHAPTER 18

# Reach for the Heart and the Head

PERHAPS THE MOST NOTABLE DIFFERENCE between managers of organizations and opponents of organizations is this: Most opponents believe that emotions are what life is all about, and that practical matters are what you have to dirty your hands with to meet the requirements of living; while managers depend on facts and consider emotions to be the gravel that gets into the works.

The extremes of these types were typified by Arthur Koestler as the yogi and the commissar.

There could hardly be a greater difference in their outlooks on life—and in their approaches to achieving their goals. And in the world of the 1980s the emotion-oriented groups have a great advantage in the process of decision-making.

Most people are a mixture of the practical-minded and the emotion-motivated. If they weren't they couldn't func-

156

tion in the modern world. But observation of what motivates their actions makes it clear that the emotions have the upper hand. It is love, passion, humor, fear, envy, greed, pride, jealousy, hate, reverence, compassion that fill most of their thoughts and motivate most of their reactions. The practical aspects of life are mostly means to attain gratification of their senses and emotions.

The overwhelming substance of the media deals with the emotions. Only in the Soviet Union does a producer try to make a theatrical movie about the glories of a tractor or the intricacies of a five-year plan. Movies, TV, books, magazines, newspapers are filled with sagas of anger, sex, pity, outrage, and other emotions. When they deal with practical matters such as business, they search for the "human interest"—how they affect family life, for instance, or "victims."

Movies and TV are composed mostly of drama, which is the milieu for immersing emotions in make-believe. Radio and recordings feature music, which is the application of sound to emotion. Art is nothing if it does not move the spirit in some way.

The way communication works in the modern world balances the fulcrum of power. It gives the less successful people the upper hand with what shapes our world—the media that form people's attitudes. People who are masters at practical matters—business executives, doctors, engineers, financiers—seem to be rewarded with stature and worldly goods. People who are inclined toward emotions and the impractical have an inside track at getting to the gears of change.

Activists tend to have a natural instinct for bringing emotion into their arguments. They avoid all the problems of reasoning out a position and strike directly for the jugular—with slogans such as "Power to the people!" and "Stop poisoning babies!"

They also have the advantage that, unlike the leaders of organizations, they need not be responsible. If it turns out that their demands have consequences exactly opposite to their intention—the way forced busing speeded the segregation of thousands of schools—so what? Will anyone sue them? Will they be fired? They know—or sense—that the media and "thought leaders" are likely to respond to emotional assertions even if there is little evidence given.

In addition to forestalling the two-easy acceptance of opponents' cases that comes from their focusing on one simplistic point or having the only input on a question, it is also necessary to raise the organization's case above the merely factual.

"Just the facts, ma'am" is perhaps the worst advice of recent years for leaders of organizations. In the arena that determines survival, the facts alone are seldom enough.

That presents a difficult dilemma. It creates the "window of vulnerability" that activists have been rushing through on scores of issues.

What makes a good executive is precisely the disciplined mind. A large proportion of executives are trained as lawyers, financial men, engineers, accountants, MBAs, and production specialists—all fields in which school grades and progression up the ladder are directly related to mental discipline—the discipline to find and weigh just the facts and not be diverted by what they wish were true, or what ought to be, or what their dreams would create. Lawyers hone their minds on the letter of the law and legal precedents; engineers on formulas; financiers on balance sheets. A law professor rightly chastises a student who ignores a volume of precedents to say that the law is as he imagines it to be. Engineers know if they deviate from the facts about materials and stress, bridges will fall or airplanes will crash.

The problem is that the audience is not discipline-minded—including lawyers, financiers, engineers, and accountants when they choose what to read in their newspapers or to see at the movies.

The first step for the executive is to accept the reality—that what has worked all during his or her rise to the top probably will not work in the public arena.

It is *essential* that the leader add to his or her retinue at least one master in combining emotion with disciplined thinking. A rare few executives have this gift or acquire it, but in most cases the combination is antithetical.

## Techniques for Moving People

Achieving the mix that can reach people's hearts and move them takes three forms:

1. *Adding emotion to logic*
This is one of the oldest and deepest bits of human wisdom. In fact, hardly any religious, business, sports, educational, government, or other function lacks devices for adding emotion that are so imbedded that no one thinks about why they are there.

Emotion is added to bolster logic in various ways:

● *Ritual.* We are familiar with the panoply of effects used in almost all religions to evoke reverence that would not be forthcoming on the basis of doctrine alone. Emblems such as the cross, raiment of the priesthood, incense and incantations, ceremonies, size and shape of churches, observances, set terminology, soaring music—all these and more are emotion-stirring supports for the doctrine. Ritual carries over to the major facts of life—baptism, confirmation, marriage, burial.

● *Recognition.* Effective leaders are aware of the power to motivate that comes from singling someone out for praise or awards. Medals, banquets, prizes—all these are nonpractical elements of organizations' functions that greatly enhance merely temporal rewards.

● *Rank.* America is supposed to be the most democratic of all societies, jealously disdaining the trappings of a class society. Yet the emotion-stirring power of rank is almost universal. It has always marked the armed forces, but it is no less vital in colleges, where eagerness for professorships stirs rivalry equal to that in sports; in companies, where the chance to become a vice-president is a spur that motivates many a rising manager; and in children's groups such as the Boy Scouts and Girl Scouts, with their pursuit of merit badges and Eagle Scout ranking.

● *Ceremonies.* Parades stir emotions so much that many people who are anti-military stand with hands over their hearts as the troops march by. Organizations go to considerable expense to mark long service of their employees with luncheons to present 25-year watches and other mementos. Recluses travel to Stockholm and don tails so they can take part in Nobel Award ceremonies in their honor.

The power of ceremonies to transcend logic is seen in memorial services, where those attending, rather than the honoree, hear the eulogy of the subject's contributions.

● *Ovations.* The need for emotion-stirring reaction to performances is seen by TV's use of studio audiences to provide applause, laughter, and other responses. The audience's enjoyment of a great concert is heightened by the applause it evokes. Hardened sports fans instinctively rise in standing ovations to recognize a great play or pay tribute to an exceptional performer when he reaches a milestone.

All of these emotion-boosters are available to the organization in building support for the logic of its case.

### 2. *Making it visible*

People have rapport with other people and are repelled by monolithic institutions. Here is another of the great divisions between activists and their targets. Activists are almost always represented to the public in the form of individuals— the Ralph Naders, Abby Hoffmans, and Lane Kirklands who hurl the charges and whose pictures appear in the media. Organizations are almost always seen as inhuman Molochs—

the Pentagon, the White House, the office tower, the administration building.

The trend toward larger organizations has accentuated this problem. The bigger they are, the more units they encompass, the less visible is the leadership likely to be among its own people and to outsiders. How many people can name the heads of the United States Armed Forces, or of the largest corporations, or of the American Medical Association?

The move toward bigness has also made organizations seem less human by appending inhuman names on them. It is difficult enough for someone to feel humanity exude from something called International Business Machines; it is far more difficult when the name is AMFAC or MoAmCo.

The ability to make something visual often wins the competition for which cause or event grasps public attention. Fifty-three hostages in Iran were visible symbols, displayed every day in the media; millions of hostages behind the Iron Curtain arouse mere murmurs. John Gacy's home produced skeletons of about 35 boys, mostly drifters, and a series of children were found dead in Atlanta. Both cases were visualized into catastrophes, while thousands of children disappear each year and get little mention.

At the height of the Vietnam War we were losing 85 men a week and the nation was wrenched. At the same time we were losing more than 1,000 people a week in highway accidents—more than half of them due to drinking drivers—and there was no outcry. It was 15 years later, when some bereaved mothers learned to dramatize their losses due to intoxicated drivers, that action began to be taken.

Activists have mastered the visual event—the sitdown, protest march, flag-burning, mass meeting. They are adept at creating stirring pictures, such as a drawing of a radiation-ravaged child or a mushroom cloud (applicable only to bombs) arising from a photo of an atomic energy plant.

## Making Arguments Visible

There are a number of ways that the position of an organization can be made more visual or dramatic:

• *Humanizing the organization.* Get articulate, sympathetic officials seen by the public through the media, at meetings, looking into the needs of the community, and so on.

• *Using ritual and ceremony.* Hold events honoring people who contribute to what the public recognizes as desirable. Give awards, trophies, citations.

• *Using television and film.* Hundreds of organizations have in-house video programs but don't get the dramatic materials about their functions out to the public.

• *Using graphics in literature.* Most people today have grown up with TV and heavily illustrated schoolbooks. They have a distaste for solid written material. They must be attracted into reading by pictures, charts, white space, devices such as • and ¶ frequently setting off key material, wide margins, and other graphic techniques.

• *Using the techniques of great writers* to create visual images in the mind. Christ used *parables*. Other devices are *examples*, such as are used often in this book to illustrate points; *analogies*, such as "The Senator's arguments for more spending are as sound as the dollar his previous programs have debased"; and *comparisons*, such as "The activists think the Treasury is a bottomless pitcher, but their arguments hold water like a bottomless bucket."

Whatever can be made to capture the imagination by becoming real forces in people's minds—actions, emotion-stirring music or speeches, films, dramatizations, events, observances, displays, or symbols—may capture public support. Ronald Reagan is called a "master communicator" largely because he is able to convert abstract concepts into mental imagery.

Words alone—still predominately the tools used by most

leaders—or pictorial matter alone—supposedly advanced technique—are seldom enough. They must "sing," create mental images, stir visualized emotions.

3. *Showing as well as telling.*

Human experience has enshrined this wisdom into one of its most durable aphorisms: Actions speak louder than words. Yet the overwhelming bulk of most organizations' arguments is presented in words.

Doing things that demonstrate the purpose and character of the organization not only breaks through into people's awareness, it also tends to unsettle the opponents. Machiavelli said 370 years ago: ". . . men, when they receive benefits from one of whom they expected only ill treatment, will attach themselves readily to such a benefactor . . ." In this more complex era it is not that simple, although the widespread support now given to George Wallace by blacks in Alabama is a recent case. But Machiavelli understood the opportunity leaders have to pull the teeth of opposition with demonstrative action.

Actions that can be taken are as diverse as the multitude of organizations, opponents, communities, issues, and other factors. Here are a few:

• Associate the organization with actions that will pull at the heartstrings: fly an ailing child to a distant hospital; show the organization's child care center for its employees' children; provide needed health equipment to people whose plight has been called to public attention.

• Expedite announcement of plans that refute accusations. For instance, reveal plans for building a pollution-free foundry if charges are made that the company cares little about the environment.

• End secrecy about the organization's good works, such as holding a Community Appreciation Day to announce the contributions to be made to various institutions and public services.

● Show how far you go to foster the public interest. Dow Chemical Canada has a large van completely fitted with the latest equipment for dealing with such accidents as track derailments or chemical fires. When the company notified the media of this van and showed it to the public, it gained credibility for its safety program. It also gained when it refused to sell an ingredient for an insect spray to be used by the government until its scientists were convinced that the end product was entirely safe.

● Identify with underdogs. Have black executives in the organization honor local black teams or students.

There are two other principles that can be used to move people:

1. *Set up counter-movements* by supporting groups that want to criticize conditions that other activists have not espoused. For instance, some organizations have provided knowledge and support for groups protesting higher costs resulting from unduly rigorous restrictions on mining, oil exploration, and other development.

2. *Don't attack opponents' views head-on.* By doing things that show they're wrong you can be more effective and avoid making them seem to be martyrs.

Attacking opponents' positions head-on puts you into a defensive position and is likely to be ineffective. The public perceives a defensive position as an effort to overcome guilt.

For example, when activists charge that a company is planning to close down a plant to avoid meeting union demands, it can be effective to move up a planned announcement of new production schedules or investment in the plant.

## CHAPTER 19

# Don't Let Them
# Set the Terms

BY ALLOWING OPPONENTS TO ESTABLISH THE TERMS used in debate we often let them dictate the terms of the final agreement.

Activists take for themselves impeccable terms that often make opposing them seem to be dastardly. Who can seem to be humane while fighting against "human rights" and "fair negotiation" and "world peace"?

They also assign derogatory names to established organizations. They hurl the epithet "Warmonger!" at anyone who advocates a strong defense establishment.

And leaders of organizations—again displaying their insensitivity to people's reactions—give ammunition to their enemies by using terms that repel people. It is hard to convince the public that leaders of corporations are greatly concerned about their sensitivities when it describes its own ideal as "tough-minded management."

So the loading of the deck on the vital ground where the terms of competition are defined is perpetrated both by the opponents and the defenders.

There are many instances in which activists have leap-frogged many steps forward by capturing that vital ground at the start.

Children who are incapable of keeping up with their contemporaries are called "disadvantaged" rather than retarded or unmotivated, to justify spending far more on them than on gifted children who could make great contributions to society.

"Disadvantaged" adults include those who have suffered misfortune and those who have never done anything to help themselves—both being entitled to largesse from the working taxpayer.

Anyone an activist group chooses to attack is called "the power structure" to imply that power is monolithic and misused. That leads to a ludicrous spectacle: a family seeking to build a two-room home in a wooded area being attacked by "conservationists" whose justification for being is to fight exploiters of the wilderness.

"Moral Majority" is widely accepted as a term for a group that represents at most one-fifth of the population.

"Public interest groups" mostly have no franchise to represent the public and advocate causes on which there is no agreement about where the public's interest lies. Public interest groups' blocking of American oil exploration contributed to the zooming oil prices of the late 1970s and the recession that followed, greatly damaging the public.

Twisting terms to deceive is endemic. "Tax expenditure" is now widely accepted as a term for the money people are allowed to keep rather than pay to support bureaucrats. Money people earn by helping finance job-creating business is labeled "unearned income." Media and others uncritically broadcast statements that government spending for the poor was being reduced, when only the *rate of increase* was slowed a little. And "the poor" is used to describe millions of people who are working, voluntarily on the loose, or living on relatives.

Success of activists in getting incorrect terms accepted as the basis for their causes has massive consequences in many areas.

Conservation was established in the United States to conserve resources and natural areas for the permanent benefit of future generations. The term "conservation" has been taken over by those who want to preserve the resources and natural areas in pristine form, of no use to humanity.

The epithet "Baby killers" was hurled at nutritionists whose work in developing excellent baby formulas had helped save millions of babies. By casting doubt on the efficacy of many types of formula, the activists frightened many mothers whose babies needed special nutrition to thrive.

Those who call themselves "the peace movement" imply that all others are opposed to peace. That enables them to start their assertions from a posture of superior virtue. "Merit employment" has been widely accepted as a description of the prohibition of considering qualifications of applicants. "Open housing" is widely used as the term for a policy that forces government-mandated housing on a community —a system closed to local preference.

In these and many other instances, organizations and people adversely affected by the usurped terms handicapped themselves greatly by allowing the terms to become established. It is difficult to forestall inroads of such terms, and it becomes increasingly difficult as time embeds them; so it is essential to challenge them as soon as they appear and counter them whenever possible.

"Wilderness" is promoted by extreme conservationists as though it were an ideal state of nature, an unspoiled Garden of Eden. Darwin and other naturalists have abundantly shown the actual viciousness that is the law of the wilderness. The Amazon and African jungles were true wildernesses before the coming of DDT and other technological innovations made them habitable for humans. But millions of Americans now uncritically accept the concept of the pristine wilderness that must not be touched by human presence.

## Creating Damaging Terms

The battle of terminology is not only being lost by default, it is also being lost through ineptitude. In many ways the leaders of organizations alienate the public through the language they use.

One of the most common errors is using war-related terms. Leaders are highly motivated to competition, and the apotheosis of competition is war. So there is a penchant for language that evokes images of war.

Strategies for nothing more harmful than sales campaigns and cost-cutting drives are called "battle plans." Employees are called "the troops" or "the work force." Executives talk about "attacking" problems and "pincer movements" against competitors. The purpose is to "annihilate" the competition. When they map a marketing program they talk of "bringing up the big guns" and having plenty of "ammunition." When they achieve a goal they say they have "gone over the top." When they plan to meet a competitor's challenge or activists' charges, they talk of "manning the barricades." Goals are described as "targets."

They feel it is forceful to say their actions will "impact" their audience rather than affect it.

And leaders wonder why the public doesn't believe them when they claim to be sensitive to the needs and feelings of people.

Just at the time workers' restiveness about being treated as humans was becoming evident—when the revolt was brewing at the Lordstown Chevrolet plant over high-speed assembly lines—industry began to talk about robots. It even coined the term "robotics" to describe the process whereby robots—"artificial people"—would take over production jobs. Instead of calling them what they are, automatic machines, it chose the far worse term. The use of "robot" aggravates workers' concerns about losing their jobs by implying they will be replaced by artificial people. That has undoubtedly slowed the workers' acceptance of increased mechanization that is vital for survival of American industry and most of the jobs that would remain after modernization.

A similar error was made that alienated much of the office staff. "Word processing" was devised in its first incarnation as a scheme for relegating most secretaries and stenographers to typing pools. In its new incarnation, involving electronic typing and computer systems, it confronts millions of people who don't want to be "processors" of anything. They want their skills and worth to be accentuated, not homogenized.

## Fight Headlines with Headlines

Terms of a dispute are often set in the headlines sought by activist groups.

Their mastery of the pungent and simplistic point not only lends itself to the media's inclinations; it even fits ideally their format for handling the news.

Every newspaper story, no matter how complex, is summed up in the headline above it. A statement by a witness before a panel that is hearing days of testimony about a complex dispute is likely to be headed:

### MANUFACTURER'S WASTE CREATES CANCER THREAT FOR THOUSANDS

The evening news will treat the report in 25 seconds, in effect pinning the same type of headline on it.

An ambitious candidate for the city council makes an assertion about a hospital's charges and the headline treatment is likely to be:

## HOSPITAL'S CHARGES
## RIP OFF TAXPAYERS

Not only does the accused face the great disadvantage of having to follow the first-day brunt of the news with a second-day response that editors give much less attention to; the response is usually an organized rebuttal of the assertion.

Such attacks can seldom be answered with even the best factual reports alone. They must be presented with equally pithy "headlines." The facts must be presented in such a way that the media have their conclusion distilled:

## CANCER RATES ARE DOWN
## IN WEST FACTORYVILLE

and

## HOSPITAL SHOWS LOSSES
## ON GOVERNMENT-PAID CASES

On the battlefront of the news media, the media's armamentarium must be used. The media start with the distilled "headline," move on to a brief summary of the most important facts, and follow with the details. *Your presentation must do the same.* The lawyer's brief or the scientist's analysis, no matter how expertly done, cannot prevail against the headline shots of the opposition.

Often the terms applied in human affairs turn out to determine the terms on which the parties settle their differences. By allowing the opponents to use their terms, and by using terms themselves that create backlash, leaders penalize themselves before the real consideration of settlement terms has begun.

Sensitivity to people's reactions to language, as well as policies and actions, is a vital element of all organizations' managements.

# CHAPTER 20

# Confound Their Strengths, Compound Their Weaknesses

THERE ARE THREE COURSES OF ACTION that an organization can carry out in overcoming opposition. Pursuing only one of them, or two, or all three may be the wisest procedure in various cases.

Even if less than the full complement is followed, however, it is wise to be prepared to conduct them all. New conditions can arise suddenly, or opportunities may be recognized as events take shape.

The three types of strategic action are:

1. *Conducting the organization's own affairs and activities to forestall or thwart opponents' efforts*

That includes a wide range of strategies, tactics, and techniques covered in this book, especially Chapters 6, 7, 8, 11, 18, 20, 22, and 23.

Organizations now may not have the option of doing nothing about their relationships with outside publics. There

**171**

are no exempt institutions, including the media and the church.

People used to be taught to respect authority; now they not only suspect it, but often consider its mere existence an affront to their independence. "Impudence" was once a common term, used to describe rare instances of someone baiting his or her "betters." It has been a little-used word the past 25 years.

Of course, the most important function occurs at the start of every consideration the organization has. Among the first thoughts on any planned action should be:

- How will various groups react to this?

- How can we initiate and conduct it to minimize the chance they will oppose it?

- Should we discuss it with them in advance and eliminate or divert their potential discord?

- Whom might they be able to rally to join them in opposition—other groups, educators, church leaders, media?

- Who might be our supporters? Should we involve them in advance?

- How should our action be introduced?

- What information and arguments should be prepared in advance? How should we disseminate them to be sure they weigh heavily in consideration given to the issue when it arises?

- What contingency plans should be made—before the action is undertaken? Cover what might happen with the media, government, constituents, and others.

- What materials will we need? What staff and outside experts?

- How will our own people (employees, stockholders, members) react to our plans? What information programs will be needed in advance? What should be done on a continuing basis as long as there is overt or likely opposition?

• How will we carry on a *continuing* program to maintain our position with the crucial publics?

At the same time, sound judgment often calls for questioning whether any action should be taken. Much of what is called for above involves *getting ready* to act, yet often the greater wisdom may be to remain ready but to withhold overt steps.

Most achievers are action-oriented. When they do recognize a problem, they tend to ask what can be done. Projections of activities, measurement, and accountability all emphasize activity. The basic questions in planning are then setting priorities and establishing cost effectiveness.

But in the human climate areas, often the crucial judgment is not activity but discretion.

When not to act . . . when to wait . . . may be the payoff decisions. Input too early is not only wasteful but uses up one's entrées. Taking a strong stand on an issue before its patterns take shape may irrevocably identify you with a rigid position, vitiating your chance to take part in the compromise when it comes. Sometimes a problem will work itself out if it hasn't been turned into a confrontation that hardens the opponent's position.

While the desire to measure results is part of good leadership, it can be self-defeating if it leads to action when discretion is better—because discretion can't be measured in a report on results.

One of the two vital qualities in human-climate matters is judgment (the other is exceptional skill in communicating). The best judgment often is knowing what not to do.

Of primary importance—whether overt action is taken or not—are functions that refute charges that opponents are likely to make. For example, an organization that has won many awards for employee safety is less vulnerable to charges that it doesn't care about the welfare of people. In all the disputes about how telephone service should be provided, there was little criticism directed at the safety record of American Telephone & Telegraph Company. It was vulnerable to charges about wage levels, promotion of women, and various intricacies of rate structure. But its well-regarded technical excellence made it comparatively immune to criticism about equipment and its handling.

Nothing makes an organization immune to attack in today's human climate. There is widespread iconoclasm even about saints and heroes. One of the most attacked systems in the country is the medical profession that is widely recognized to be the world's best and that has made medical wonders available to most people. But the odds against being attacked can be reduced and the effects made less virulent by having antennae sensitive to how people will react and by following the kind of judgment, planning, and actions covered in this book.

The second form of strategic action is:

## 2. *Undermining opponents' strengths*

Most of the strong points that activists bring to bear in a dispute with an organization are also vulnerabilities.

● Their strong affinity for emotion can make their appeals effective, as we have seen, with most people and the media. But emotion often overrides logic in leading them to take their stand. That makes them vulnerable to a sound, carefully documented, and effectively orchestrated program that erodes supporters' sympathy by washing away their flimsy foundation.

● *They are prone to simplistic approaches that coincide with people's penchant for simple answers.*
That works so long as the issue remains simple. When it is demonstrated to be complex, with various sides and especially with potentially undesirable consequences, people who respond to the simple tend to lose their concern and withdraw their support.

● *They have little need to study the subject and research the facts.*

When they grasp an issue they look only long enough to find "evidence" that supports their position. Months or years of investigation are avoided; manpower is not devoted to gathering and sifting information. Even more important, they don't have to weigh evidence that complicates the matter or refutes their position.

That advantage becomes a vulnerability when responsible judges can be prevailed on to review the entire issue. When a group that called itself Public Advocates came up with a 200-page report on infant formulas it at first made a great impression in the media. But when the report was demonstrated to be filled with misinformation, distorted statements, non-existent reference sources, and naive misinterpretation of scientific findings, its stature with scientists, government, and major media plummeted.

● *They have no need to be responsible.*

Activists face almost no consequences for being discredited. The worst that can happen to them is that they will find it a bit harder to be taken seriously in their next campaign. Robert B. Choate, the civil engineer who gained brief fame with his charges that breakfast cereals were useless nutritionally, has attracted no further fame since the absurdity of his charges was established. (There has recently been some thought of suing the leaders of unfounded attacks for harmful mischief; but since it would be costly and there would be little prospect of collecting damages, the purpose would be more psychological than substantive, so little legal action has been taken so far.)

Again, this advantage can be made to backfire. After a number of Ralph Nader's attacks—including some on Congress—proved to be irresponsibly hollow he found his next campaigns getting less and less attention. Members of Congress and even many media people labeled him a "hip shooter" and he found the caliber of his guns diminished.

● *They appeal to Americans' sympathy for the underdog.*

Activists are almost always careful to present themselves as people without resources or influence—"little people" boldly taking on the behemoths of The Establishment.

By focusing on how Nader had built a conglomerate of well-financed agitating groups, his targets were able to deprive him of his cherished underdog role. All the publicity about how Spartanly he lived and how little his people were paid because of their dedication evaporated when he refused to reveal how much was spent. Similarly, Common Cause proved to be far less effective than it expected because its expensive ads and highly visible posture gave it the image of a big "people's lobby."

● *They can apply a lot of unpaid time to the cause.*

While the supporters of the organization are busy in their jobs, usually including much more than 9-to-5 schedules, activist groups often can draw on hordes of people with nothing more exciting to do. People who find little to stir them in their work and little to make them feel their lives make a difference are ready recruits for crusades to be carried on after working hours and on weekends. Non-working wives whose children are in school or married, while less numerous than before, are still a large pool for recruiting of volunteers. College students—especially those not studying demanding courses such as medicine, engineering, and business management—usually make up an active portion of activist cohorts.

This is a formidable advantage, but it means that most of the opponents have not demonstrated they can be successful in competitive situations. They embody all the weaknesses that are open for the organization to compound.

## Putting Pressure on Their Weaknesses

The third form of strategic action is:

3. *Compounding opponents' vulnerabilities*
Besides the vulnerability that accompanies each of their

strengths, there are other weaknesses. These are in addition to whatever deficiency there may be in their cause.

Each of them can be spotlighted for review by the media, government, and the public through the techniques we have discussed.

● *They are likely to be weak at organizing.*

This is partly because of the natural selection that takes place in a free society. People who are strong organizers tend to be attracted to working *within* organizations, where their talents will be rewarded. Those who dislike the systematic thinking and attention to detail that make a good organizer dislike organizations—and are likely to be prospects for activist groups.

Dissident groups tend to create impressive-looking structures, with layers of positions and lots of room for accommodating egos. Such groups tend to be houses of cards when the pressure is needed to get things done.

● *Their emphasis on passion usually leads to fuzziness in structuring their course.*

The literature of activist movements is full of frustration over their inability to meet unexpected challenges, to go beyond the first step or two of their strategies. That is a major reason many movements have floundered in their endless debates about goals and principles.

Alinsky said: "One of the great problems in the beginning of an organization is, often, that the people [who join it] do not know what they want."

He recognized that it is inherent alienation looking for a cause that leads many to become members of a movement. The concept of the cause attracts them but they are fuzzy about what they really want to happen. So long as the purpose seems to be clear, they are enthusiastic. When it ceases to light them like a beacon their dissidence begins to stir unrest.

By requiring the activists to confront new barriers—particularly those that require accommodations within the movement—this weakness can reduce the movement to impotence.

● *Their messianism makes them short of patience and discipline.*

When early success is not achieved, the restiveness that marks many dissidents comes forth. They need periodic victories and few frustrations. Also, the need of many dissidents to feel they amount to something cannot be satisfied for long by being just one of a group; they already have that in their jobs and their neighborhoods.

They tend to be disaffected and self-centered.

Dan P. McAdams, a psychologist at Loyola University, Chicago, in 1983 studied 72 radicals and 88 moderates of the '60s. He found that the radicals showed significantly more interest in power (using others) and significantly less interest in both intimacy (warm and harmonious relations) and achievement (concerted work toward a long-term goal).

" 'Power to the people' was once a radical slogan," *Psychology Today* commented. "The radicals seem to have meant themselves."

These traits bring to bear on the group the discontent that underlies most members' taking part, and especially the discontent of those with a drive to correct "evils" their way.

That is why virtually all activist movements have a high rate of dropouts and are marked by splintering into rival groups. Either by purge or by voluntary withdrawal, movements tend to segment. The original Russian Bolsheviks had their Trotskys and Stalins. Other activist groups also tend to spin off rival groups that vent their scorn on the progenitors as well as on the organizations they both oppose.

This inherent tendency of most activist groups to divide offers opportunities for their targets to conquer.

● *They lack leaders with the needed strengths.*

Organizations have learned that they need different types of leadership at various times in their development. First needed is the innovator or entrepreneur. He or she must be succeeded by the organizer and planner. And then must come the administrator/manager.

Movements also have changed needs in their leadership, but often they cannot make the transitions.

At first there is likely to be a person who articulates the idea and identifies the cause. Only rarely is that person also suited to fill the next role, the messianic inspirator of faith and enthusiasm. And that mover of people rarely is suited to going on to be a manager of affairs for a large and complex movement.

Sy Kahn, a writer who participated in mass movements, listed 20 traits and 16 skills that he believed the effective leader of a movement needed. Clearly, one who has the first few traits faces a major personal challenge—and the movement faces a crisis—when each new set of traits and skills is required.

At each of these stages the movement is vulnerable. It is at these seams in its development that the breakaways are most likely to occur and the frustrations to mount.

● *In sum, they are weak at getting things done.*

All the traits we've examined add up to a very low efficiency ratio. While an organization deals with its issues and communications with a few dozen people, at most, many movements ingest the time and energies of thousands. Where they achieve all or a major part of their goal, it is most often because 1) they had such a meritorious case they should have been accommodated at the start (see Chapter 6) or 2) their targets failed to use the judgment, tactics, and skills that overcome opposition.

Each activist group will show these weaknesses in different degrees. It is important that its target assess its *bête noire* to determine which vulnerabilities to work on.

That calls for early and careful assessment of the group—observing, but not planting spies. Explore thoroughly all you can learn about their coterie of leaders. People involved in the group are often eager to discuss their concerns with friends, neighbors, writers, and others. Their publications are seldom secret. Some media are likely to report what they say and do. Dropouts from the group talk about their reasons, and especially what's wrong with the leadership.

Remember that they count on you either to play by gentlemen's rules or to overreact and gain public sympathy for them. Alinsky, David Dellinger, and other philosophers of dissidence based much of their strategy on the assumption that leaders of established organizations will pursue conflict as gentlemen, to avoid looking combative in their polite circles.

Change the limitations of gentlemanly combat enough to interfere with the one-directional course they are counting on.

Upset their equilibrium by doing unexpected things, such as counter-rallies, repeated delaying tactics, lawsuits, provocations of their latent jealousies, and discrediting of their materials. Such tactics are mild compared with the unrestrained tactics they are accustomed to using.

# CHAPTER 21

# Focus on the Decisive 10 Percent

THERE IS A WIDESPREAD MISCONCEPTION that to influence public opinion it is necessary to reach all of the public.

Underlying that is the simplistic view that since there is "public opinion" there must be "a public." Actually, of course, there are many publics. One person is simultaneously a member of many—a woman, a mother, an employee, a member of a given church, a Republican, a resident of a community, a taxpayer, a supporter of clean air legislation, a lover of the wilderness. a Norwegian-American, and so on.

Her viewpoint will be a part of the climate of opinion of any of these publics—and she will strongly oppose on one topic the same person she strongly supports on another.

The opinions of each of these publics will involve great variations among those who comprise it. Among women, for instance, there are many ardent supporters of abortion and others who are activists in opposition to abortion. And still others have opinions of various shades in between.

Another basis of misconception is another result of the penchant for putting things into neat packages. "Public opinion," since it is known to have great powers, is visualized as an entity. In this age of computerization and measurement, it is assumed that any entity can be measured. To be measured, an entity must be definable in some specific terms, such as volume or numbers. The philosophy is: If you can't count it, it doesn't count; and if it doesn't count you don't have to account for it.

The public's growing awareness of public opinion polls has led further to the simplistic feeling that opinions can be pinned down like butterflies and measured.

Actually, public opinion is never a truly measurable entity like an election vote or even as firmly expressible as belief in God. Practical-minded people, feeling nervous with matters that cannot be pinned down and evaluated, have a strong tendency to equate public opinion with numbers in a printout.

This ignores such factors as intensity of opinion, timeliness, direct concern about the question to various individuals, and so on.

If the minority of anti-abortionists are intense while the majority favoring liberal choice for pregnant women are less so, "public opinion" may be perceived to lie with the minority. Public opinion may be almost palpable on a question such as tax cuts, or scarcely detectable on reciprocal trade agreements. A woman may say she favors a lid on hospital charges on her wedding day and again a week before giving birth —but not with the same intensity.

So in approaching the question of how to affect public opinion, it is vital to understand what public opinion is not.

It's not a still picture but a constantly moving picture. Any poll—even if valid—merely captures the respondents' viewpoints at one instant in time. Days or even hours later— or after some influence has had an effect—the pattern may have changed.

Public opinion may be as changeable as cloud patterns. Winds or even breezes of ideas and influences can alter it. Like clouds, they may be soft and benign but then be built up by stormy winds of argument into thunderheads ready to burst.

Public opinion is weighted and distorted by intensity as well as immediacy. A small minority of rabid advocates for closing down nuclear plants may prevail over the vast majority who passively approve them.

Public opinion varies infinitely with the importance of the subject, the viewpoint of the interpreter, and the makeup of the public involved.

It's vital to recognize that any public is made up of members, and that the members interact with each other. They affect and are affected to varying degrees by all those in the group. Inevitably, how they feel about anything at a given time is as much involved as a slice of onion in a pot of soup.

A member of any public is caught up in the human climate, just as a lake is caught up in—and affects—the natural climate. Opinions around each person affect his or her opinion, as well as reflecting it.

So most of the time *public opinion is not really what people think. Public opinion is what people believe other people think.*

It is this interflow of influences that determines how opinions change. And that requires spotting which elements within a public are the germinal points.

It is not the whole amorphous public that must be reached but those germinators and movers. They start the process that leads to the majority perceiving what "people believe" and thereby make it their belief.

## The Bell Curve of Influence

Major attention should be focused on the "swing" portion of the public being addressed. On almost any issue the range of attitudes tends to follow a bell curve (Figure 21-1).

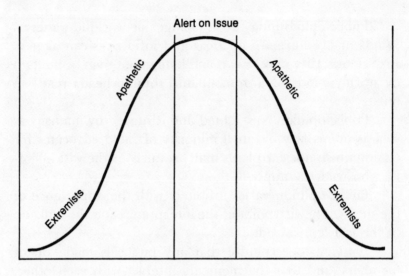

**Figure 21-1**

At each extreme there is a small group of perhaps 5 percent who are entrenched in their views.

Perhaps 40 percent on each side of the spectrum are apathetic or inert on that issue.

That leaves perhaps 10 percent who are in the "swing" group—those who take an active interest in the subject and are open-minded. Whichever viewpoint has a majority of that 10 percent leaning toward it tends to prevail in the climate of attitudes on that subject. *A swing of 2 or 3 percent among that group can reverse the leanings of the total.*

The zeal of many people at each end of the spectrum becomes zealotry. They do not base their attitudes on reason or the evaluation of information. Thus it is useless to try to reason with them.

Zealots maintain their zeal only so long as they feel they have the material and psychological support of others—constituents, parishioners, media, or masses among the apathetic who think little about the subject but lean toward the zealots' position.

When constituents cool in their support, the small band of zealots is isolated and its momentum wanes. The zealots become isolated and, except for the lunatic few who may resort to violence, are neutralized as a force.

The swing of opinion among the small segment who generate attitudes serves to redirect the apathetic mass who were leaning toward the extremists' position. That's why changing the leaning of that alert segment emasculates the effectiveness of rabid extremists who are so visible when attention is focused on their clamorings.

The effect of shifting the alert group is to permeate the populace, shifting the mild leanings of the great mass of the apathetic and cutting off the effect of the vocal extremists by withering away their climate of support.

The momentum of an opinion is like centrifugal force—pulling the whole in a direction without strongly moving the whole.

## The Direction of Opinion Flow

It is this pattern of influence—in which the predominant leaning of opinion becomes what the public at large perceives to be the consensus—that determines whether a change can be effected.

When the weight of opinion is moving in a direction opposite to what an organization desires, it is unlikely that efforts at persuasion will succeed. The current of opinion is flowing strongly in the opposite direction and the fragile tools available cannot reverse such a tide.

However, when the tide is shifting it is eminently possible to speed up its movement to the desired direction by getting into the flow of impressions and pushing them.

For example, for more than 30 years American businesses and conservative organizations sought to convince the public that the trend toward massive government and handout programs hurt the nation's economy and character. They had no visible effect.

When the consequences of those policies began to be visible to people, however, the trend began to shift. The alarming rate of inflation due to government deficits; the alarming decline in ability of American industry to compete with foreign producers; the moral dissolution resulting from conditioning millions of people to demand more and more handouts—these began to lead people to question the established course.

Then the economic education and persuasive efforts began to show effects. Arguments and techniques that before had done little to stem the tide now served to speed up the realignment of public attitudes. The audience's posture of receptivity had gone from nil to responsive.

That is the formula for effecting a change in opinion: the combination of the alert group in the bell curve who determine the weight of opinion and the susceptibility of attitudes to messages that are in tune with people's receptivity at the time.

Accordingly, the best strategy calls for avoiding head-on opposition to entrenched or emerging opinions. Instead, find an aspect of the subject that you can support and that the public is receptive to. Then you can build open-mindedness and acceptance, from which you can watch for opportunities to broaden the audience's readiness to listen.

For example, the right of property owners to turn away tenants' applications for any reason went unquestioned for centuries. Efforts by Jewish, black, and other minority groups to arouse public support for laws prohibiting discrimination got nowhere. Then, after World War II, landlords, enjoying a vast demand for houses and apartments, discriminated against many veterans and young couples with small children. By focusing public attention on these problems rather than aspects the public was closed-minded on, advocates of anti-discrimination laws were able to get a hearing, made the issue one that legislators found it politically fruitful to pursue, and succeeded in getting laws passed.

## Influencing the Alert Group

The pattern for shifting the viewpoint of the alert group includes:

1. Identify the 10 percent who are to be the target, keeping in mind the segmentation that exists within all groups. That calls for identifying them by various traits:

- *Self-interest in the subject.* Who are the ones with something clearly to gain?
- *Intellectual level.* Who are the ones who grasp the seriousness and nuances of the issue, who can articulate it to others, whose thought leadership will get others to follow?
- *Local.* Are there certain areas where the issue is particularly pertinent, such as a region dependent on certain jobs, or one where a health concern is prominent? Are there areas where the media are already receptive, and whose influence can lead to getting media elsewhere to pay attention?
- *Group membership.* Are there certain bodies, such as churches or civic organizations, where members of the alert segment are concentrated? Are there some whose position is already the same as yours and who can be rallied into a coalition?
- *Sex.* Is the issue primarily of interest to one or the other?
- *Age.* Similarly, to one age group or another?

2. Efforts should be concentrated on the prime groups, resisting the temptation to disperse resources by trying to reach, at the start, a broad base. When you have momentum built and your position is in the spotlight, with little added effort the spectrum of coverage can be broadened.

3. Get your position embodied into the context of the audience—part of their thinking. That can be accomplished by (1) tying all messages to what's in it for the audience; (2)

getting them involved so it's *their* effort too; and (3) making the communications theirs by communicating *with* them, not *at* them. Don't preach, lecture, admonish, threaten, frighten, or otherwise try to impose on them what's on your mind.

4. Use a variety of channels and media. When someone hears an opinion expressed by a dozen people it has much more influence than when he or she hears it twelve times from the same person.

When a multiple combination of messages impinges on one's attention, the impression is created that the idea is all-pervading, that it is "the thing to do." It therefore has considerably greater influence.

The same number of messages is likely to be far more effective if they are directed through many channels— television programs, radio commentators, newspapers, motion pictures, word-of-mouth discussion, club meetings, sermons, and other channels—than repeatedly through the same means.

5. Be consistent. There are no walls that separate what one group of people hears from what reaches others. Blue collar workers hear what is said to executives. Men hear messages directed at women. Seeming to make contradictory or inconsistent statements gives the impression of duplicity. That destroys the credibility that is essential to keep the support of any audience.

Just as the persuasive effort is focused on the pivotal segment of the public, so should be the monitoring of how opinion is changing and the persuasive effort adjusted accordingly.

# SECTION FIVE

# Getting the Desired Result

# CHAPTER 22

# Organizing and Operating to Overcome Opposition

BEFORE A PLAN IS UNDERTAKEN for dealing with potential or existing opposition, it is vital to realize that every situation must be approached afresh. It is possible to establish guidelines, but not blueprints.

Every organization differs from all others in its own character, the functions it performs, the localities it functions in, the areas in which it is likely to confront opposition, its allies, its enemies, and many other factors.

Every situation is different from all others because it occurs at a different time and usually with many varying conditions.

That caveat is essential to prevent mistakes before establishing suggested structures and functions. If strategies and tactics were chosen on the basis of a fixed checklist, mistakes would be as inevitable as if one chose eyeglasses from a random assortment.

There is no "one size that fits all" in any aspect of human relations, and particularly not in the multifaceted and explosive area of opposition between dissidents and organizations.

It is also essential to maintain flexibility. Conditions within each organization change constantly. Its functions and operations change.

The climate of people's concerns changes. One year it is most agitated about inflation, the next about dealing with unemployment by undertaking steps that cause inflation.

The susceptibility to activists among decision takers—legislators, bureaucrats, judges—changes.

Conditions may change in one area and not in others. Drought may make policies on water use a hot subject in two or three states while the rest of the country gives them a low priority.

Every organization needs to take a diverse approach to its needs. Many have dug themselves into a Maginot Line on one issue, only to be overrun by another issue it had not heeded soon enough.

Breadth of approach is vital to see the opportunities facing the organization as well as the problems. Emphasis on combating opposition and meeting issues can lead to a negative frame of mind or a siege mentality.

There are many opportunities to forestall an issue by eliminating a potential source of attack, gaining the support of potential opponents in advance, or winning allies for still-unfaced struggles.

An important function in combating opposition is forming coalitions of supporters. Preventing opposition may make it wise to join coalitions *formed by others* who have had the foresight to detect early warning signs.

Short-term perspective must be combined with long-term scope. Most movements take two years or more to become active concerns, so a long-term view is necessary. Programs and resources for the long haul must be established. But it is a mistake to set up firm programs on a long-term basis (and in today's climate one year may be long-term). Structures and programs given firm charters for a long period may not be alert to the nuances of change; and they may fail to take advantage of opportunities and to make vigorous responses to unexpected developments.

The problems to be faced will almost certainly be new to the organization's staff. They will probably require considerable diversity of mind, as well as experience. The organization—no matter how able its people—is unlikely to have those traits. A decision-making group composed of tangible-minded executives, all employees of the same organization, is likely to reinforce its myopia and prejudices, rather than resolve them. One or more experts with great diversity of experience, objectivity, and creative judgment are essential.

## Getting Organized

All elements of the organization that will have dealings with outside groups or will be affected by them—which means virtually every department—should be involved. The knowledge of each is important for the perspective it can apply. And how the organization deals with an issue will affect all of its elements. Effective handling, in fact, is unlikely unless all of them are constantly aware of the development and course of the issue.

This means that although dealing with opposition is a function of the head of the organization, it is also a function of any executive anywhere in the structure to sound alerts when signs of dissent are seen. Any executive should be able to make inputs of knowledge or recommendations. Anyone should be encouraged to provide information about activist groups or work with members they know through college, church, or community contacts. And any executive can demonstrate his or her value to the organization by making contributions to the thinking and actions that resolve an issue.

That is an important point. Coping with mass attitudes means having as many points of view and as many points of contact as possible. *It is a responsibility of top management, but it is a function of everyone in the organization. And it is a means toward advancement that may not show on the usual personnel records, but may be more important for the health of the organization than most of the usual bases of measurement.*

The structure may be a formal one, such as a Task Force on Issues and Opportunities, or informal, involving merely a web of interchanged communications and occasional discussions. In either case, one or more people from each major segment should be constantly involved. In the case of a corporation, they would include:

- Office of the president or chairman
- Corporate planning
- Operations
- Finance
- Marketing
- Production
- Law
- Government relations
- Public relations
- Human resources
- Outside counsel

This combination of viewpoints and backgrounds can provide as nearly a fail-safe network as can be formed. It is most likely to bring up every foreseeable consideration and to have every feasible action reviewed and critiqued. Internal jealousies and conflicting ambitions are likely to be accounted for and neutralized.

A process of constantly monitoring all sources of inputs should then be set up, either within the group or as an assignment of staff people.

Monitoring should include all sources that have a bearing on the organization's functions. It should especially include those sources that are not normally seen by the executives. Those sources might include:

- The underground and "alternative" press.
- Learned journals that carry the early musings and trial balloons of activist intellectuals.
- The intellectual press, such as *New York Review of Books*, *Commentary*, *The Atlantic Monthly*, *The New Republic*, *The Nation*, *Rolling Stone*, and *New Leader*.
- Periodicals of various activist movements, such as *The Crisis*, which reaches blacks, and *Modern Maturity*, which is read by elderly people.
- Books that raise alarm about some alleged evil, such as Rachel Carson's *Silent Spring* and Ralph Nader's *Unsafe at Any Speed*. Even more indicative may be the reviews such books get in the intellectual publications and major newspapers.
- The programs of societies composed of sociologists, radical economists, and other social engineers.
- Applications to federal agencies for research and study grants.
- Emerging complaints that show up in the mail to Congressmen, state and local legislators, and government agencies.
- The organization's own mail and telephone calls, which often can flag emerging concerns well before they burst out as issues.
- Comments of the organization's employees or members, who are a constant antenna for the messages being sent out by their neighbors and associates.

## Preparations on Each Issue

When a grievance has been spotted as a possible emerging issue, procedures should be undertaken on an "early warning" basis. These include:

1. Analyze the reasons for the grievance. Is there something wrong with the activities of the organization—a problem of quality, of explanation, of service? Is there something wrong with the role of suppliers, dealers, service organizations, employees or members? Is there a gap in communication, poor exposition or presentation?

2. Analyze the source of the grievance and the nature of the people who make it. The considerations in Chapters 4 through 6 should be reviewed.

3. Study all the facts about the subject of the grievance. Review all reports and documentation. Discuss the matter with experts within the organization.

4. Review outside reports and sources: government, other comparable organizations, associations or coalitions, libraries, suppliers.

5. Make an objective analysis of present attitudes about the grievance: in government, among competitors or other comparable organizations, among critics, in the public media, in specialized journals.

6. If the climate is unclear, conduct opinion surveys as further clues, among groups affected by the grievance, among various activist groups that may become involved, among employees, among stockholders or members.

7. Determine what others affected by this grievance are doing. Avoid duplication; coordinate, form coalitions, assign responsibilities.

After this research has been evaluated, the organization's position on the subject can be established. That may include changing procedures, policies, or positions. If so, the effect of those changes should be monitored to see whether the early growth of grievances abates or they must be kept on the docket.

In either case, the organization's position should be written up and explained to everyone in the organization who may have any bearing on the subject.

## Identifying the Publics

When a grievance emerges as an issue being pursued by one or more activist groups, the process of dealing with it must go on to further stages.

First is making up a list of all the publics that are to be dealt with and operational means for dealing with each.

The list of publics will vary for each organization. In the case of a large corporation it will include:

- Employees. They may be reached in toto on some occasions or by groups at other times, such as executives, operating staff, subsidiaries' staff, and the local plant and office level.
- Government. These lists will be broken down by elective and appointed officials, and at the federal, state, and local levels.
- Financial community.
- Stockholders.
- Customers.
- Prospective customers.
- Unions.
- Suppliers.
- Plant and office communities. These may be broken down into community leaders and the public at large.
- Academia. Separate lists may be devised of those who are specialists on the issue (such as chemistry, biology, or law) and all other academics.
- Other opinion leaders—churchmen, civic groups, women's organizations, Parent-Teacher Associations, and so on.
- News media. These are likely to require many lists, covering national, regional, and local; various types of editors and producers; columnists; editorial writers, and others.
- Other media. Included may be books and reference works that deal with the issue or aspects of it; specialized publications that deal with the subject or the organization's field of activity; the alternative press.

With the structure established, the research done, and the audiences worked out, attention should focus on what's to be done—or at least what should be in readiness in case it is decided to take action.

Several functions should be undertaken before there is any clear indication that a problem has emerged into a threat:

1. Prepare an authoritative document on the issue that can be the key source for everyone who is concerned with it. It should emphasize the key points and highlights, with the bulk of supporting information used as backup documentation. (See Chapter 18.) Make the material as inviting as possible.

2. Either distribute it or be prepared to distribute it, through personal contact wherever possible, to affected government officials and personnel, colleges, journals, public media, other interested organizations, associations and societies, and libraries.

3. Designate which officials of the organization are to be constantly briefed on this issue or opportunity. Establish the lines of authority to be followed and the communications channels to be used.

4. Prepare those officials for tough questioning by the media, in confrontations with activists, in testifying to committees, and in conducting meetings.

5. Prepare fact cards on the issue and the designated officials of the organization (with their home phone numbers), for distribution to the media.

Other functions may have to be carried out if the issue surfaces enough to call for concerted action. As much as possible, preparations should be completed in advance. Then they should be selected and carried out expeditiously and professionally:

6. Prepare testimony to be delivered before governmental bodies.

7. Set up an emergency plan for each local unit of the

organization and on each potential issue. It should include the line of authority, designated personnel to deal with each likely function, and facilities for the media at the site where action may occur.

8. Statements should be prepared as responses to charges made by opponents or in response to potential questions. They should be concise, punchy, clear, and quotable.

9. Plans and facilities for press conferences and television coverage should be set in advance.

10. Readiness for preparation of press releases should include having all factual materials available at every possible site, typewriters or word processors, facilities for reproducing releases and photos, and telecommunication or mail facilities.

11. Fact sheets and illustrations should be prepared in advance, for distribution to the media if needed.

12. Videotaping facilities and provision for making copies of videotapes should be set up, or a fast source identified, in each location. Videotapes should be used for recording events, as material for TV stations and for the organization's own dissemination, and as a deterrent to media distortion by providing a record of actual occurrences and statements.

13. Brochures and other literature should be written and dummied up, ready for final revision and printing.

14. Bulletins or letters should be prepared to reach employees immediately with explanations of the issue and the organization's position.

15. Inclusion of this type of material in all employee publications and video news programs should be planned.

16. Notices should be prepared for bulletin boards.

17. Advertisements that present the facts—in a direct and non-combative tone—should be prepared in preliminary form. They might include insertions in major newspapers, newspapers in localities where the organization is active, publications of opinion leaders concerned with the issue, and publications reaching members of the opposition group. TV and radio commercials should be prepared for possible

placement with local stations that accept editorial-type commercials.

18. Letters and literature addressed to key customers or supporters should be roughed out.

19. Letters to stockholders or members should be prepared in preliminary form.

20. A list should be readied of the various public platforms that may be available for spokesmen of the organization, and speeches should be drafted for delivery by designated officials.

Throughout this process of action and readiness, schedules should be set up with priorities, time requirements for completion of each function, and the time needed for clearance and approval of various materials.

Flexibility must be maintained to allow for unexpected developments and changed emphases. That means that all schedules, assignments, and budgets should not be made firm. Some things may become unnecessary and others may arise at any time. Parameters for expenditures can be set at the start, with limits that cannot be exceeded without specific authorization.

It is important not to assume the attitude of siege or war, but there is much similarity between a campaign on an activist issue and a battle. Alertness, fluidity, readiness to change position, constant review of tactics, thrust and counterthrust, knowing how many resources to commit without over-committing—all of these are necessary.

# CHAPTER 23

# How It Adds Up

THE SHIFT OF POWER AWAY FROM LEADERS OF ORGANIZA-
TIONS is a struggle to determine who shall make critical decisions. Should they be made by the people who are supposed
to have responsibility for the organization and the consequences of its actions? Or should the leaders be relegated to
ceremonial custodians carrying out directives of people who
don't deal with the intricacies and have no responsibility for
the results?

Management by activism, in this light, becomes aban-
donment of responsibility for society's institutions.

The previous chapters have examined the conditions
and requirements for preventing this arrogation of authority
by those who will not have responsibility. It is useful to summarize the key points that the organization's leaders should
observe.

The very strengths that have created masterly managers

make them especially vulnerable to the tactics of dissidents. Running complex organizations requires the skills of disciplined people who focus on facts.

However, the requirements of the sophisticated organization are being changed by imprecise elements that don't fit that pattern of information. Issues created by public attitudes are causing managers their greatest troubles. The masterly manager is trained to maximize certainty by focusing on reports, balance sheets, and other forms of measurement. The world in which the organization must function is marked by constant upsets, impacts, and other uncertainties. (See Chapter 3.)

Precisely because those who become activist opponents of an organization are different in their background and approach it is essential that the executive work to understand them.

The starting point for overcoming opposition is recognizing the depth of its roots, and then understanding the nature and motivations of opponents.

There are four basic types of opponents. They are inherently different and require different treatment in the organization's responses. They are:

1. Advocates, who propose something they believe in.

2. Dissidents, who tend to be sour on things as they are and include a given cause among the things they are unhappy about.

3. Activists, who are restless with things as they are and want to press for a cause—which may be changed for another cause when the first one loses their interest.

4. Zealots, who tend to be single-minded and unable to see things in perspective or to countenance compromise or accommodation. (See Chapters 4 and 15.)

There are, of course, many cases in which the advocates of changed policies or practices may be right. It is wise to approach with an open mind each instance of outside requests for change, or even with an eagerness to learn from them.

Many of the best suggestions received by any organization originate with outsiders who see a better way. Much can be gained from recruiting the brightest and most sensible of them, both to gain fresh blood and to convert them to your side.

Remember that you can deal with reasonable and moderate critics, while extremists' positions are vulnerable. North Americans are a temperate people; they are repelled by any excess. In a free society every excess creates its own demise—or at least gives you openings to thwart extremists' efforts.

Basically, there are two kinds of pressure aimed at changing organizations and institutions—persuasion and force. Persuasion leans heavily on the merits of the case, though it also involves emotion and simplistic approaches. Force depends on frightening people. Few groups in America have gained their goals through fear or force. Americans get their backs up when they think they are being coerced. If your opponents use force, that is an opportunity to reverse roles and become the underdog. On the other hand, avoid even the appearance of using force or coercion. (See Chapter 6.)

Activists have learned to preempt the agenda for their causes by capturing the stage first and dictating the script. As a result, public issues have often been forced into public consciousness and then pushed through the entire agenda of "consideration" to a conclusion without all the facts or the true consequences being considered.

In an age of electronic immediacy and visual impact, always having to *react* to others' initiatives is to seem *reactionary*.

A defensive position is, therefore, a position of weakness —in tactics and in the eyes of the people.

Taking the initiative to fill information vacuums and to confound the thrusts of opponents can avoid being put on the defensive. Make sure that sound information on the organization's position is working to prevent charges of opponents from being taken unquestioningly by opinion leaders and the media. That can go a long way toward your being perceived as a porcupine instead of a lamb. It can discourage attacks and weaken the virulence of those that are made, tending to send the dissidents looking for a more recumbent target. (See Chapters 8 and 17.)

So it is vital to control the agenda of public consideration on an issue. (See Chapter 7.)

## How to Prevail

Orientation of leaders must start with understanding the viewpoint of the audiences. The crucial point in preventing opposition is to bite your tongue before you say "we" and train yourself to say "they." When talking with others, the question is "What do you want?" not "How can we get what we want?" We're most likely to get what we want if the publics feel their interests are being addressed. (See Chapter 10.)

By training and inclination, the current generation resists reading anything that is not concise and inviting. Yet the training of most leaders is in lengthy exposition. Brevity, visual markings that set off key points, illustrations and charts, summaries—all these and other techniques are required to get attention for even the best case. (See Chapter 11.)

In addition, persuading people requires combining emotion with logic. The overwhelming substance of what interests the people and the media involves the emotions.

As a result, people inclined toward emotions and the impractical have an inside track at getting to the gears of change. It is necessary for the executive to acquire mastery in combining emotion with disciplined thinking—either through new training or by adding a master in that ability to the retinue. (See Chapter 18.)

Countless confrontations have been fueled with ammunition provided by the organization that was being attacked. Don't give ammunition to your enemies.

Activist opponents need conflict not only to achieve their goals, but to keep their supporters together. By turning provocations into conflict, organizations often provide their enemies with precisely what they want most.

And they need victories—even small ones. The great majority of dissidents have few victories in their lives. The hunger for "achievement" is an attraction of the activist group. Its absence turns people off. So avoid appeasing groups with victories that they can exploit to pursue bigger demands. (See Chapters 12–14.)

Activists, like the public, like to oversimplify. They isolate one point in highly complex situations and declare *that* is the problem. Forestalling and fending off such attacks requires preventing opponents from isolating their simple answer and getting all attention focused on it.

Opponents' simplistic charges must constantly be put into their full context. By constantly showing the small role the alleged problem plays in the full context, you not only weaken their case but raise the doubts of the audience by filling the vacuum in which it is comfortable for them to form a judgment. (See Chapter 16.)

When there is a vacuum of information, the simple accusation or slogan stands alone in consideration of the issue. That has the effect of transforming an assertion into the "information" on the subject. The public mind grasps it like a frog snapping up a fly—and slams shut.

So the primary strategy in forestalling opponents' efforts is to fill the information vacuum. Nature abhors vacuums but activists love them. Become the most authoritative source for information and make it available to all those who have a role in developing thought on the subject—before opinions begin to jell on the basis of slanted input from opponents. (See Chapters 6 and 17.)

By allowing opponents to establish the terms used in debate we often let them dictate the terms of the final agreement. Activists often take for themselves impeccable terms that make it difficult to oppose them. And many organizations create terms that provide opponents with evidence to support their charges.

By allowing the opponents to use their terms, and by themselves using terms that create a backlash, leaders handicap themselves before the real consideration of settlement terms has begun.

Sensitivity to people's reactions to language, as well as to policies and actions, is a vital element of all organizations' management. (See Chapter 19.)

To maintain stability in the face of unsound attack, organizations should avoid the pitfalls of their leaders' inclinations; they should take advantage of the opportunities provided by the nature of the opponents.

Dissident organizations have strengths that can be thwarted and weaknesses that can be exploited.

Do not counter their thrusts head on; deflect their force and give yourself the initiative. That will deny them the benefit of their strengths, of setting the agenda, of establishing the terms for the competition. (See Chapters 16 and 20.)

The arena in which most of the fray will be contested is the communications media. The media have become more important as gatekeepers of the public agenda than as actual creators of change. But they are vital in resolution of most conflicts and most of the time their inclinations favor the opponents.

The mass media are like cameras that are supposed to provide a picture of the world. What a camera reproduces may be only a small part of the real world, or a distorted picture of it. So it is with the media.

So understanding the media and knowing how to make sure the pictures they provide to the public are clear, representative, and fair is crucial. (See Chapters 8 and 22.)

Leaders of organizations have responsibilities—to those who employ or elect them, to their staffs, their communities, their profession, their country. They are responsible for maintaining and advancing the organization's ability to fulfill its functions. That means they must assume the responsibility of maintaining stability while evolving and improving. An evolving and improving organism cannot be bettered by being disrupted.

So today it is a primary responsibility of the executive to thwart those pressures for change that are unsound, impassioned, misguided, based on cupidity, or otherwise inadvisable—and to overcome that kind of opposition.

It is a matter of survival—for each organization and for our society that is built on the effective functioning of the organizations and institutions that comprise it.

# INDEX